A GUIDE TO INT

ONE COUPLE
TWO FAITHS

stories of love and religion

Marion L. Usher PhD

ADVANCE PRAISE FOR
One Couple Two Faiths: Stories of Love and Religion

Marion Usher is a powerhouse, a visionary, and an inspirer, not only of the couples whose lives she has changed, but also of religious and other leaders who make a difference in the lives of communities. When I first decided to counter the prevailing mindset in Conservative Judaism and speak out for interfaith couples and families, it was Marion who became my support and mentor. Her brilliant insights about the lives and needs of interfaith couples helped me to shape a vision for a synagogue that not only welcomes interfaith families, but also actively works to integrate them into the fabric of our communal and religious life.

>Rabbi Gil Steinlauf, Senior Rabbinic Advisor
>Adas Israel Congregation
>Washington, DC

Marion Usher's *One Couple Two Faiths: Stories of Love and Religion* is a must-read for all who care about the future of American Jewry. She has been at the forefront of challenging us to create an inclusive Jewish community where interfaith couples are welcomed, respected, and supported. With personal insights and practical strategies, she raises important questions, shares compelling stories, and celebrates what is possible.

>Paul Entis, Director, Jewish Food Experience
>Rockville, MD

We need more Marions in this world—those who not only talk about interfaith inclusion, but those who really *get* how to make it happen. This book is a gem because it isn't about preaching—it's about sharing stories that can help us all understand the realities of what it means to be "inter-anything."

>Laura Conrad Mandel, Executive Director
>Jewish Arts Collaborative
>Boston, MA

One Couple Two Faiths is of equal relevance to interfaith couples and their parents. We're all grappling with the challenge of living with difference. We must marry our differences elegantly. This is that guidebook of inspirational candid testimony.

>Ari Roth, Founding Artistic Director
>Mosaic Theater Company of DC

Without diluting or simplifying the issues and stresses—and without losing faith—Usher draws on her therapeutic practice and presents realistic strategies for a multifaceted, and still Jewish, family life.

>Dr. Carol Zemel, Professor Emerita, Art History and
>Visual Culture, York University Toronto, Canada

This book is an invaluable resource for interfaith couples, clergy and congregational leaders. Dr. Usher has shared some of the most intimate stories of couples on their interfaith journeys. As someone who often works with interfaith couples, I look forward to sharing the lessons from this book with them.

>Rabbi Esther Lederman, Director Congregational Innovation
>Union for Reform Judaism

One Couple Two Faiths hits all the buttons — how to navigate interfaith marriages that respect each partner's background, how to have loving and accepting conversations around family traditions and dynamics, and ultimately, how to create a new paradigm for Jewish practice in an interfaith family. I wish I had a resource like this when I, the product of a non-observant, interfaith family, made the decision to embrace my Jewish identity and create a Jewish home and family when I got married 25 years ago.

>Karen Paul, Executive Director
>Tikkun Olam Women's Foundation of Greater Washington

Through beautiful and honest stories and reflection, *One Couple Two Faiths* charts a course through the struggles people face navigating religion as they build a home together.

>Jacob Feinspan, Executive Director, Jews United for Justice
>Washington, DC

Marion Usher is a gentle listener who truly understands through her many years of work and deep caring about individual families that we as a community need to be more inclusive. She reminds us that no family should be left on the sidelines of desire to engage in Jewish life in an open and accepting embrace.

>Carole R. Zawatsky, CEO
>Edlavitch DC Jewish Community Center
>Washington, DC

Marion Usher has spent countless hours listening to interfaith couples providing them with techniques to address the challenges stemming from their different backgrounds. Her wisdom helps couples and their extended families realize the incredible opportunity presented by every intermarriage.

>Mik Moore, Principal
>Moore+Associates, New York

Dr. Usher has opened the Jewish communities' eyes to the potential in each interfaith couple to build and expand our Jewish family. She offers tangible advice, anecdotes and suggestions for wading through this reality as a community, clergy, individual or couple, built upon her experience of listening to couples as they struggle to find their unique path.

>Andrea Deck, Director of Engagement
>Honeymoon Israel, Washington, DC

ONE COUPLE
TWO FAITHS
stories of love and religion

Copyright © 2018 Marion L. Usher PhD

ISBN: 978-1-62429-148-7

All rights reserved. This book or any portion thereof may not be reproduced or used in any manner whatsoever without the express written permission of the author except for the use of brief quotations in a book review.

Published through Opus Self-Publishing Services
Located at:
Politics and Prose Bookstore
5015 Connecticut Ave. NW
Washington, DC 20008
www.politics-prose.com / / (202) 364-1919

This book is in honor of the interfaith couples and families who have worked with me, shared their stories, and who, in these workshops, have experienced the Jewish community through an inclusive lens. Thank you for trusting me and for being part of my life.

TABLE OF CONTENTS

Foreword by Edmund Case
Introduction
Four Questions Interfaith Couples Need to Address

Chapter 1
JEWISH JOURNEYS
    Jacey and Aaron
    Matt and Melissa
    Adam and Liz
    Margie and Michael
    Leigh and Jeff
    Lisette
    Marcia
    John
    Michael and Maria
    Andrew and Tara
    Blanche and Daniel
    Tommy and Susan
    Howard and Sandy Marks
    Summary

Chapter 2
WHAT IS JEWISH IDENTITY?
    The Expanding World of Jewish Identity
    Transmitting Values Through the Holidays
    We Don't Celebrate St. Valentine's Day!
    An Evening of Storytelling
    Going to the *Mikveh* for Conversion
    A Path Toward Conversion
    Gugu's Jewish Journey and Thurza's Baby Naming
    Creating a Jewish Identity Within an Interfaith Family
        Through the Generations
    A Canadian Learns about American Thanksgiving
    A Random Meeting at Open City Café
    Summary

Chapter 3
WORKSHOPS – A MAP AND A PROCESS
- Should I Attend "Love and Religion: A Workshop for Jews and Their Partners"?
- Through Thick and Thin
- Is This Really the Last Dance?
- "Love and Religion" Workshop Reunion
- An Enlightened Community Creates New and Welcoming Projects
- Conference on Cutting-Edge Programming for Interfaith Couples
- Workshop for Parents of Young Adults in Interfaith Relationships
- Workshop on Raising Young Jewish Children
- Workshop on Intentional Grandparenting
- Summary

Chapter 4
FAMILIES AND HOLIDAYS – CONFLICT OR OPPORTUNITY
- Thinking About Rosh Hashanah
- It's Either Too Early or Too Late
- The Day After Thanksgiving
- Honoring Christmas in a Jewish Interfaith Family
- Surrounded by the Magic of Christmas
- Actually, Santa is Jewish!
- Christmas in Vermont
- Thinking about Passover
- Where is Baby Moses?
- Five Ideas for Creating a Meaningful Seder
- What is the Hardest Part of Passover for Interfaith Families?
- Three Tips to Personalize the Passover and Easter Holidays
- How Would Hogwarts Host a Seder?
- Summary

Chapter 5
THE NEW JEWISH FAMILY – CONTINUING THE JOURNEY
    Making Effective Programs for Interfaith Couples and Families
    What Do Interfaith Families Want from the Established Jewish Community?
    Being Religious is Only One Way to Identify as a Jew
    Is Outreach Effective with Interfaith Couples?
    This is What Outreach Looks Like
    Engaging Interfaith Couples Through the Arts
    The Wonder Twins
    Presentation to the Board of the Jewish Federation of Greater Washington
    Summary

APPENDIX
    Description of "Love and Religion" Workshop
    Book List
    Acknowledgements
    About the Author

FOREWORD

I am so pleased to honor and congratulate Marion Usher on the publication of her book, *One Couple Two Faiths: Stories of Love and Religion*.

Since close to the time that InterfaithFamily got started as an independent nonprofit in early 2002, Marion has been a leading and valued partner in efforts to engage interfaith families in Jewish life and community.

In 2004, Marion and I spoke on a panel at the DCJCC's Jewish Film Festival, discussing a film on interfaith marriage. In 2009, we spoke on a panel at the DCJCC again. This time it was for the premiere of Marion's wonderful documentary film, *Love and Religion: The Challenge of Interfaith Relationships*.

In developing the "Love and Religion" workshop, Marion was a pioneer. Since 1994, countless couples have made Jewish choices for their family life and their children as a result of participating in her workshops. Marion was one of the first to realize the impact that is possible when interfaith couples are gathered together under Jewish auspices to discuss their religious life together, and in particular, the power of building relationships between the facilitator and the couples, and between the couples themselves.

In 2007, when InterfaithFamily convened almost every professional in the country then working to engage interfaith families, Marion was a featured speaker, educating participants on the importance of couples workshops.

After InterfaithFamily grew from being a web-based content resource, we piloted an online offering of "Love and Religion," facilitated by Marion, and included a version of the "Love and Religion" workshop in our 2011 program offerings for interfaith couples.

Today, interfaith couples continue to benefit from Marion's approach, not only in Washington, DC, but also in "InterfaithFamily/Your Community" projects in Atlanta, Boston, Chicago, Los Angeles, Philadelphia, and San Francisco. One of the key takeaways at the 2016 first-ever Interfaith Opportunity Summit was the importance of relationship building in engaging interfaith families, validating precisely the approach Marion has been promoting since 1994.

Marion has also been a leader in working with interfaith couples and families at her own congregation, Adas Israel, and has provided an example of how Conservative synagogues can welcome and engage interfaith families.

Her book focuses on personal stories, as told through the eyes of interfaith couples as well as Marion herself. It is this intimate aspect that makes this book so valuable for the Jewish community. Here, interfaith families, congregations, and the greater Jewish community can see how inclusion is accomplished.

Something I said in my comments back at the 2009 film festival is still true: Marion Usher is a "jewel" that the Washington, DC community—and the national Jewish community—is very lucky to have.

Edmund Case
Founder of *InterfaithFamily*

INTRODUCTION

My work with interfaith couples was inspired by a discussion I had with my husband, Michael, twenty-five years ago. "The Jewish community is making a serious mistake in ostracizing interfaith couples," he told me. "Furthermore," he added, "if the Jewish community included these families, it is obvious that we would have more Jewish children." He suggested that I was in a perfect position to create a program for these couples, given my commitment to and involvement with Judaism as well as my many years of experience as a therapist, helping couples and families work through their problems. His support was essential to this process, since I had failed to anticipate the negative response I would receive from the Jewish community.

At that time, my suggestion to reach out, welcome, and include interfaith couples cast me in a complicated role. Clergy and national Jewish organizations were preaching in-marriage—Jews marrying Jews—as the only solution for countering the ever-increasing rates of intermarriage. In 2013 the Pew Research Center study reported that among non-Orthodox Jews who were married, 72% were intermarried. This was a major increase since the 1990 National Jewish Population Study where 52% of Jews were intermarried. Even with these rising numbers, welcoming interfaith couples into the Jewish community was unthinkable.

I believed a different approach was needed. From my clinical experience, I knew that early intervention could make an enormous difference, and I developed a workshop, "Love and Religion: A Workshop for Jews and Their Partners," for this purpose. In a safe environment, interfaith couples could work through the issues that are inherent in an interfaith relationship. They could listen to other couples facing similar conflicts. They could be vulnerable in front of each other as they examined the role of religion in their lives, constructed a religious life for themselves and their children, and learned essential skills for building a successful marriage. In our sessions, couples reveal their worries, concerns, and dilemmas. They ask each other questions. They feel accepted in a group of peers.

Whenever I talk about my work in this field, the first question I am asked is, "Why did you create these workshops?" followed by the assumption, "Oh, you must have intermarried children." My answer is always the same. "My husband and I are Jewish, and both of our children married Jews. I do this work, because I want more Jews in the world."

I grew up in a Conservative Jewish home where Shabbat was celebrated every week. My mother grew up in poverty in the Osterpole, Ukraine, better known as "The Pale of Settlement," and reinvented herself when she immigrated to Canada in 1920. She taught herself how to make a beautiful home, cook delicious food, and impart her love of Judaism. She taught us Jewish values through her own acts of loving-kindness. Collecting clothes, raising money, and doing good deeds for others was part of her daily life. She was beloved by all her friends and the entire synagogue congregation.

My father, in addition to appreciating her efforts, focused on building the Shaare Zion Congregation in Montreal, the synagogue in which I grew up. He had little formal education and took in the world with his eyes and ears. When he realized the significant relationship between an excellent Jewish education and Jewish continuity, he spearheaded the campaign for our synagogue to build the first Solomon Schechter Academy, a Hebrew day school in Montreal.

While no one I know would call my father a champion of women's rights, he was enthusiastic when Rabbi Maurice Cohen, our rabbi, suggested that I have the first bat mitzvah in a Conservative congregation in Montreal. And so, on a Friday evening in December 1953, I stood up at the *bimah*, gave a *dvar Torah,* and chanted the *Haftorah*. This experience affirmed me as a Jewish woman and empowered me as a young adult.

Judaism was the center of gravity in our family. I loved being Jewish. Values were transmitted through a Jewish lens, celebrations centered on Jewish holidays, ethnic food was reinterpreted through kashrut, and religious observance was carried out through our synagogue affiliation. We were a typical "made-it" upper-middle-class Montreal Jewish family of the 1950s. I wore cashmere sweaters, went to summer camp, and attended a mostly Jewish public school that closed for all the major Jewish holidays. We lived surrounded by Jews; people on the street who were not Jewish and not like us were invisible. Decades later, I realized how many populations were invisible to us: French Canadians, Blacks from the Caribbean, WASPs, and all who weren't like us socioeconomically. It was too complex for my parents to include "others." They were too preoccupied with creating a good life for us. It's what they did best.

In that community, an interfaith marriage was seen as shameful. When our good friend married a Protestant woman in 1962, his family sat *shiva* as if he had died. In that era, conversion didn't make it any easier. The convert to Judaism was still seen as "less than."

Now, as I work with interfaith couples and help them create a religious life together, my own Jewish heritage is integral to the process. My love of Judaism encourages these couples to consider raising their children as Jews. As practicing Jews, we have the Torah, a moral code of behavior that teaches us that it is our responsibility to make the world a better place, an intellectual tradition, and we are known as the "People of the Book." We have a commitment to family and to the world around us. All these values are worth preserving.

In 1977, when Rosalyn Yalow was named a Nobel Laureate in Medicine, she was asked what being Jewish meant to her. "Even in the face of persecution and dispersion, and often denied entrance to centers of learning, the Jewish people, never satisfied with conventional answers, have always valued intellectual inquiry and continued to honor wisdom and learning," she replied. For her, Judaism represented a great synthesis of universal and Jewish values. Rabbi Ephraim Rubinger in *Why Remain Jewish* by David C. Gross, points to being Jewish as intellectually challenging, ethically rewarding and offering a lifestyle replete with joy and happiness. He does not want to break the 4,000-year chain of Jewish life and history. Neither do I.

I am writing this book because I want to share my experiences with interfaith couples in their journeys toward creating their religious lives. These are stories written by the couples themselves. They address the already complex subject of love complicated by an interfaith relationship. At their core they are stories about struggles and about the path—ultimately—toward a Jewish identity.

I am grateful for the couples and families that let me into their lives. How do couples from disparate backgrounds find their way through the maze of feelings and tensions that religious differences can provoke? I have learned that the answers come from the couples themselves. There is no one correct formula. Each interfaith couple is special and different. Each couple decides for themselves. It is my hope that they feel affirmed and supported in the decisions they make as they establish a religious home for themselves.

My hope is that those couples who choose a Jewish life will experience the same joy and happiness it has brought to our family.

FOUR QUESTIONS INTERFAITH COUPLES NEED TO ADDRESS

These questions emerge from my clinical experience, the process in the workshops, and the couples themselves. When answered, they create the framework in which the couples can move forward in their decision-making process. As a therapist, I am committed to helping couples acquire the skills necessary to build a rich marital life. The first question outlines some of the basic principles, which, when incorporated, provide a functional way of communicating as well as crucial skills for constructive problem solving. The other three questions are specific to interfaith couples and their concerns.

1 How do you build a successful marriage?

I strongly believe in premarital counseling for all couples prior to marriage. As such, I offer couples in the workshop two complementary approaches that provide the framework on how dynamics function in their relationships and how specific ways of communicating can diminish or enhance their marital life. "I think that these skills allow you to have those difficult dialogues you don't want to have, to talk with other people, and to think about those issues. My grandfather used to have a saying that if we spent half as much time planning our marriages as we did our wedding, there'd be a lot less divorce. I think about that phrase, and it's true. This work helped us prepare how we were going to lead our life as a married couple," the spouse of one of the couples observed.

The first model is based on the concepts of "attachment and autonomy." Attachment exists between two people when each feels he or she can absolutely rely on the other person. It is an emotional state in which each partner understands that they are available for the other and feel unconditionally safe with one another.

Autonomy, defined as "all that we do to take care of ourselves," refers to how we function in our family and work lives, how we manage our internal life, and how we take charge of our independence. In our lives we need to feel attached to our partner as well as feel we can be our own person.

When one of these dimensions supersedes the other, the relationship can become dysfunctional.

The second model, based on the work of couples' therapist Dr. John Gottman, led to the development of a template describing the factors and behaviors that make marriages functional. He outlines which processes are malignant to a marriage, which are helpful, and what couples can do to improve their relationship. These processes are presented in his book *Why Marriages Succeed or Fail*. One of the best resources in the field of couples therapy, it identifies criticism, contempt, defensiveness, and stonewalling as the four malignant processes that erode a marriage. He offers four strategies for repairing the damage: calm down, speak non-defensively, validate, and over-learn. These concepts are easy to comprehend and are very helpful to couples as they learn how to live together.

I have found these two models, characterizing how healthy couples relate, to yield fruitful conversations. As couples apply these newly learned skills and concepts, they often focus first on their parents' mode of operating. As they become more comfortable with revealing their own issues, they go on to talk about their own dynamics. They appreciate having these new tools and skills for looking at their own ways of operating.

2 Where does an interfaith couple go to find help?

Interfaith workshops are hard work, but they enable couples to acquire the skills they need to create their own religious observance in their new home. Participants meet other couples who are worried about similar issues. They find answers to their questions and experience the value of a protected environment where confidentiality, empathy, respect, inclusion, and open discussion are all respected. In the workshop, couples talk about issues related to their families of origin, the part religion played in their growing-up years, the type of religious education they received, and the religion in which they want to raise their children.

Anna and Craig have known each other for more than six years and have already celebrated both secular and religious holidays with each other's families. They were contemplating marriage and had not been successful in resolving their religious differences. They were at a loss as to how to take the next steps and where to go for help. "When we found a 'Love and Religion' workshop on the DCJCC website, we were so excited. It was just what we were looking for. It really helped us with some important conversations we needed to have about our future life together. It empowered Craig and me by validating all the work we have done to reach this point and confirmed that we had more to do. We also loved meeting other couples who were dealing with similar issues and challenges. My fiancé, Craig, and I were recently engaged and hoping to get married next spring. We needed to start thinking about the ceremony, our parents, and our different religious backgrounds. In this group we received more help than we could have imagined."

Information for interfaith couples is now readily available online. The most frequently used website by interfaith couples, Interfaithfamily.com, provides many support systems, such as clergy, workshops, community events, and blogs to fortify interfaith couples in their process. In smaller cities where there may not be an ongoing "Love and Religion" workshop, clergy or a couples' therapist can be sought for counseling. Additionally, individual couples themselves can seek out other interfaith couples in their communities, friend groups, or by the way of the Internet, and host a group discussion. In this informal setting, they, too, can experience the protection and support of a group dynamic, while expressing personal and shared challenges.

3 How will religion inform your lives as a couple?

The salient question every interfaith couple needs to answer is, "Will we practice both religions equally, or will we choose one religion to be the *lead religion* in our home?" I have coined the term *lead religion* because it describes a challenging reality: the existence of two religions in the home. Even when there is a conversion, there are still two religions between the extended families, since each person comes from a different religious background and parents and grandparents, aunts, uncles, and cousins come from and celebrate different religions. Embracing a lead religion means practicing one religion in the home, while still respecting the other. This is an approach that both honors and acknowledges the other religion, a vital decision for any interfaith family.

"Adam was Jewish, and I was raised Mormon. We grew up in Salt Lake City, Utah. We had known of each other our entire lives and were reacquainted on a flight home for Thanksgiving for a truly Hollywood-style story. Our interfaith marriage class greased the wheels of conversation for both of us. After each class, we felt comfortable talking about such challenging issues as children, families—and Christmas," said to me by Merilee, Adam's fiancée.

Choices, we know, always involve losses and gains. In an interfaith relationship the losses stem from the fact that each person comes from a different cultural and religious background and cannot share the easy familiarity of having grown up in the same religious experience. The acknowledgement of this difference and of the loss of similarity is the first step in the decision-making process. Gains can only emerge as the couple grapples with defining the question "What will religion look like in our home?"

The questions are numerous, often starting with how we talk to our parents and families about the decisions that we are making concerning our religious lives. How do we decide about our wedding? How do we deal with the reactions from our friends and families?

Often individuals come from families where religion was an integral part of their lives. Therefore, it is reasonable to assume that they, too, will want religion incorporated in their home. Consequently, a central issue for them, and all interfaith relationships, will be to make choices and to decide precisely how religion will be practiced in the new family they are establishing.

4 How will you construct a religious identity by which to raise your children?

Couples decide on how they will construct their religious lives out of their family-of-origin's practices, their belief systems, and their own values. These complex topics need to be explored and examined within a framework of mutual acknowledgement and respect. Each of the partners is encouraged to express their own thoughts, feelings and beliefs. The couples who have attended my workshops find this session on religious identity to be among the most helpful.

For example, in one class, a participant shared with his girlfriend for the first time why it was so important for him to have his children raised as Jews. Before coming to this workshop he had been reluctant to tell her how the basic tenets of Judaism informed his daily life, and how important it was for him to continue this tradition. Because of how he was raised, and the fact that his grandparents were both Holocaust survivors, he wanted to have a Jewish home. The need to move the relationship forward propelled him to reveal his innermost thoughts and emotions while allowing his girlfriend to hear and understand how strongly he felt about raising their children Jewish. His courage opened the door for her to tell him about the enormous loss she would experience should she choose to give up her religion and join him in Judaism. Clearing the emotional pathways helped them to make decisions that were desirable for both of them.

The task for each partner is to explore their own religious identity and background and to talk about what is possible for them as individuals, as a couple and in the future, their children. By listening with empathetic ears to their partner, they will be able to envision together how religion will inform their lives.

Interfaith couples explore different scenarios as they continuously construct a religious identity for their family. Whether they have these discussions by themselves, in a workshop, in a therapeutic setting, or with a member of the clergy, the issues to be discussed are the same. Will we establish a *lead religion*, or will we practice both religions equally? Will we join a religious institution? Which holidays will we celebrate? How do we help our families support our decisions? When I am asked, "What do you think?" I tell them that this is all very complicated. The exciting thing is that as an interfaith couple, they can create something that is unique to them. The question they have to answer is whether a religious identity is important to them. When the children are raised with one religion, they can then identify with that group and participate fully in the communal life of that religion.

How different couples answer these questions is told in the stories throughout this book. Interfaith couples will read about similar situations to their own, and see how couples resolve their struggles. Interfaith couples and their families will learn to successfully navigate this complicated process and find a religious path appropriate for them.

1

JEWISH JOURNEYS

Every couple has a story about how they met. As a therapist, I want to rekindle the attraction each person has for the other before we get into the work that needs to be done in the office. With all interfaith couples, I ask the same question of what attracted them to the other person. Here I want them to realize that religion is only one part of their lives. Their love and their connection are the most important ingredients that hold them together. It puts religion into a place where it can be worked with and not seem like a deterrent.

Storytelling allows us to reveal our innermost thoughts, to show our authentic selves and to take an audience along with us on our journey.

Through these stories, interfaith couples can identify with the storytellers as they share their conflicts, struggles, and resolutions. I aim for them to be affirmed in their concerns, worries, and yearnings. While every interfaith couple's path is different, there are common elements for all.

One of the hardest parts of a relationship is to reveal your secret thoughts and wishes to your partner. Everyone's fear is that they will be confronted with rejection, disappointment, misunderstanding, or hurt feelings. Often, periods of contention in a relationship develop when a partner feels disconnected because of something they are withholding. For interfaith couples, there is commonly an internal struggle to share the importance of one's religious connection and the role they hope religion will fill in their lives together. Most of us know well what it feels like to fall in love as well as to feel disconnected and distant.

Dissonance can occur when we do not yet know what we want, but we recognize an existence of difference. There can be hesitance and fear to communicate these feelings of conflict because they are not fully formed and can push away the other person. How we grapple with it, present it, talk about it, and attempt to close the gap is a necessary process. Is there a possibility of working this out? Problem solving becomes the central focus of the relationship at that point. By working together toward a resolution, the space for love returns. This is what these stories are all about.

JACEY and AARON

JACEY   I was raised in the Northern Virginia suburbs right outside of Washington, DC. Both of my parents are Jewish, and we grew up relatively traditional. We were members of a Reform synagogue, observed all of the holidays with our large extended family, and I spent a number of summers at a local Jewish camp. From a young age, I was strongly encouraged to marry someone Jewish; in fact, I felt downright pressured at times.

AARON   I grew up in the mountains of western North Carolina in a mostly non-practicing Presbyterian family of artists. I had little exposure to Judaism; in fact, I knew only two Jewish people and very little about the religion.

JACEY   Aaron and I first met at the University of North Carolina. I was the date of one of his fraternity brothers at a party, and we talked for a while. Then I didn't see him again for ten years, until we met again at a party in New York City.

AARON   I recognized her, but wasn't sure from where. She didn't recognize me, but we hit it off immediately.

JACEY   Once we became serious, we realized we had a lot to figure out on the religion front. We were lucky enough to find out about and enroll in Marion's interfaith workshop, which was an empowering and pivotal part of our journey. It really helped us with some important conversations and decisions about our life together. In addition to meeting other couples like us, the class helped us realize that although it could be painful at times, we had the power to chart our own course. Just because it didn't look like how we were each raised didn't mean it wasn't right or beautiful.

Chapter 1—Jewish Journeys

AARON   Conversion was not for me, but I supported the fact that Jacey wanted to raise our kids Jewish. And while our three children now identify as Jewish, we honor the holidays of both of our religions. We joined Temple Sinai in Washington, DC, a synagogue that welcomes and embraces interfaith families. In fact, I drive our eight-year-old son Benjamin to Sunday school every week.

JACEY   We joke that half the members of our congregation aren't even Jewish. We just love that everyone is welcome, and we feel very at home in this community.

JACEY and AARON   The life we've created together has been different than either of us predicted, but better and more rewarding than we imagined. We hope to model for our kids that differences don't have to create division; in fact, if you let them, they can make life more interesting and enriching. It's all about compromise, open-mindedness, and putting your relationship first. However, the earlier you can work through these decisions, the better off you'll be down the road.

MATT and MELISSA

MELISSA   My coworker fixed us up. Matt was a childhood friend of her husband. She had witnessed several relationships run their course and thought we might get along well. Neither of us had been set up before. We did *not* like each other when we first met. We did *not* like each other after our first date. Nor did we like each other after our fourth date. Yet, here we are—married seven years with six-year-old twins.

We are the unlikeliest of couples. I was raised in a Jewish home by first-generation Jewish parents. I grew up in New England, a middle child with brothers on either side. My father is a physician. My mother worked out of the home. We went to private schools. There was never a time we didn't know we would go on to college. My parents divorced when I was fifteen. We spent free time in bookstores and libraries and running around outside. Jewish holidays were large celebrations. So, too, were birthdays, Thanksgiving, and any occasion my mother felt like celebrating.

My husband is the youngest of three, with an older brother and an older sister. He claims North Carolina as home, but as the son of a career Marine, he moved around a lot as a child. Education was not a priority in his home. He joined the Marines out of high school. He was raised Catholic and was an altar boy as a child. Birthdays and holidays were days on a calendar, often unnoticed events. Sports, playing and watching, were the times of family "togetherness" and conversation. The first hug my husband had from a male adult was from my father.

My husband tells people I proposed on our second date. I didn't. What I did do was ask him if he would be open to raising Jewish children if he were to marry someone Jewish. To him, this was tantamount to getting on one knee. To me, this was about not wasting my time dating someone I would eventually have to break up with because raising children anything but Jewish was out of the question for me. Not only do I identify as Jewish, I also have a deep commitment to my heritage and to those family members who lost their lives in the Holocaust, and bringing Jewish children into the world was going to be my way to make sure they did not die for nothing. I was not insistent that my partner be Jewish, just that he be open to having a Jewish home and a Jewish family. Matt was OK with that.

Matt said he had fallen out with the Church several years prior when he was working to start a nonprofit organization focused on human trafficking. When he approached his church for a donation, he was told that funds were going toward a new organ instead. He could not make sense of this. It seemed to go against the teachings of his youth. He walked away and never looked back.

When we decided to get married, the rabbi we approached to perform our ceremony insisted that we take an Introduction to Judaism course together, which she taught. Matt was fascinated at the diversity of the couples in our group: mixed race, homosexual, transgender, and different faith couples. He was routinely caught off guard by the fact that one of the fundamental parts of Judaism is to question everything—so different than his Catholic upbringing. He found it…liberating. This was one of the main reasons he chose to convert two years ago, along with his desire to share the same faith of his wife and children.

The "big" things like our wedding, children, *bris*, kosher home… these were easy. It was, and is, the small, or smaller, things that have proven to be our greatest difficulties. Not having a Christmas tree in our home. My not finding Jewish jokes funny—ever. Understanding that Israeli and Jewish are not the same thing. Not working on the High Holidays. And then there are the really small things that we bump up against regularly. The things you cannot exactly explain, that just come from the fact that I was born Jewish and raised Jewish, and he was not. He will never know what it was like to be the only Jewish child in class on a regular basis. To routinely be the first Jewish person someone has met. He cannot know how it changed me to have been one of two Jewish families in our Vermont town or to be told so often, "You don't look Jewish!" not knowing what that meant.

We got into a fight recently because I overreacted to a comment he made about not wanting to reveal that he was Jewish to an Arab individual he had just met. When I am out and about in the world, on some level I am guarded/prepared for offhand remarks that might offend me. But when I am in my home, my guard is completely down, so I am jolted easily in a way I could not explain to him. I have lived my entire life as a Jew. He has been one for barely two years. It seems our greatest challenge is my giving him the space to internalize what it means to be Jewish and time to live life as a Jew, and his greatest challenge is finding a way to walk in my shoes until he is comfortable walking in his own.

ADAM and LIZ

ADAM At the outset of any relationship it's hard to say where things will lead. It's easy to push off discussion of possibly controversial topics like religion until they become problems. For Liz and me, the idea that our religious backgrounds could be a source of conflict first came up several months into our relationship, but was somewhat glossed over until our engagement. In the run-up to our wedding, we both faced pressures and expectations from friends and family, straining what should have been a blissful time.

We knew we needed help. So we did our research and reached out to Dr. Usher for private counseling. We then registered and took part in the "Love and Religion" workshop. It helped us to take a step back, evaluate our needs and desires, contextualize outside pressures, and understand how to best deal with them and each other. Conflict became an opportunity to listen, learn, engage, and grow.

The workshop helped us acquire the insight, tools, and strategies necessary to address interreligious issues in our wedding and beyond. We have now been married almost six years, and we recently celebrated the birth of our first child. We are so grateful that we took the time to explore these issues and created a religious life that works for us.

Since our marriage, we have learned to be more open to each other's family and faith backgrounds. Instead of seeing our differences as challenges, we try to see them as opportunities to learn something new and seek common ground. After all, the Abrahamic faiths, in our view, have more commonalities than differences.

One key to our success has been conceptualizing our shared religious practices as concentric circles. The two of us are the center of the circle, our parents are the next ring out, our extended family and friends the next, and so on. When exploring new situations we start from the position of "What works for both of us?" If a practice only works for one and not the other, or if it's something done to please a family member at the expense of one of us, it's simply a non-starter. This can be challenging for any new couple as you create your own circle and exert greater independence from your parents, but ultimately we've found it necessary to assert the primacy of our own family unit and ensure that we are making decisions that support and affirm our relationship first.

For example, we recently had our first child, a beautiful and healthy baby girl, and we were able find ways to honor the baby in both of our families' faith traditions. We did a naming with the cantor at my synagogue, and we did a blessing with a priest at Liz's mom's church. Both were lovely events with attendance and participation from both families, and most importantly, they were events that we were both comfortable with. We had examined more traditional options, like a baptism or a more religious naming ceremony, but we chose to do what felt right for both of us. Our unity helped our families to accept, understand, and appreciate our choices, and it helped us to smoothly navigate what could have been a difficult issue.

MARGIE and MICHAEL

MARGIE   Michael and I attended the "Love and Religion" workshop in the spring of 2014. We were in the somewhat unusual position of having welcomed our first child Jonah in May 2013, but not yet being married. We also were excited to learn that we were expecting a second child that fall. We decided to sign up for the class after seeing it advertised in the DCJCC weekly email. The birth of our first child had made it clear that there were opportunities and challenges that we needed to explore as an interfaith couple and understand how that would impact our growing family.

We were excited to meet the other couples in the class who had interesting and diverse religious backgrounds, ranging from Buddhist to Catholic to all types of Judaism. While we were the only couple that already had a child, two other couples were expecting, and all others anticipated having children in the future, so the issues of how to navigate this situation were salient for all of us.

We looked forward to the class each week, where we could explore interesting questions about important traditions, beliefs, events, and so on. Some of these we had already encountered, and others were on the horizon, but each allowed us to reflect deeply on how we could co-create a meaningful way of honoring our respective backgrounds, families, and values.

Michael and I each took away some important thinking from the class. Michael recognized how challenging it was for me to participate in his Orthodox congregation, and we have since worked to identify other ways that our family can connect to Judaism while allowing him to maintain this relationship to an institution that is deeply meaningful to him and his family. For example, we have participated in a greater number of activities at the JCC, which has been a welcoming and open place for our interfaith family. I identified some helpful ways to ensure that my extended family feels welcome participating in Jewish events, including inviting them to share holidays with us. We continue to honor their Protestant traditions as well.

I recognized that while I have never felt fully comfortable with formal religious practice, the traditions, rituals, and values can be deeply meaningful. I can already see that our children are excited to connect to

Judaism in numerous ways. They love to say *havdalah* on Saturday nights, they like to help make challah, and they enjoy saving money in their *tzedakah* box to help others.

We have since gotten married, with Dr. Usher officiating, in a lovely ceremony with important Jewish elements, including a *ketubah*, a *chuppah*, and a modified Jewish ceremony as well as a secular poem read by my father, which allowed my family to feel included as well. Our wedding was very meaningful to both of us and had elements that were important to each of our families.

It hasn't been easy, but we have managed to craft our own interfaith path through honest dialogue, mutual understanding, and a deep respect for each other's traditions and values. Now with three boys, we continue to navigate the complex, but fulfilling experience of an interfaith family raising Jewish children.

Leigh and Jeff

Leigh We are thirteen years into it, and I hope not close to the end. Please realize that we see ourselves as a work in progress, and we are just here to share our choices and experiences. To continue the metaphor of the journey, the most important thing for you to understand about us is that we did not embark on this journey with a fistful of pamphlets from a travel agent and a set itinerary to get us from point A to point B efficiently. We were more like the people who travel to an unfamiliar land, wander around, go down a few streets, and get lost a few times, not knowing the language or understanding the currency. In other words, we were a couple of bumbling idiots. But that turned out to be excellent preparation for the adventure of parenthood.

For us, as with many interfaith couples, our first main hurdle was the wedding. Priest? Rabbi? Both? Neither? Who might we alienate in our families, and how much should we worry about that because, after all, whose wedding is it, anyway? In the end, we chose to avoid the issue and elope. We had a civil ceremony at the Palazzo Vecchio in Florence, Italy. That was during our dramatic phase. It was lovely, and it resembled none of the weddings ever held in either of our families. We were married in a country that is historically Catholic, and it was a few days before Christmas, so one of our pictures is of us in front of the glittering Christmas tree in the hotel lobby. But it has also struck me that the iconic picture from that day, the one that we most often show to people, is a picture of us in our wedding gown and suit, sharing a kiss, with Michelangelo's colossal statue of David as the background. So the way I see it, I was not the only Jew present for my wedding day.

We drifted through those first few years of marriage, learning what it means to make a life with another person. We negotiated through various holidays, but then I got pregnant, and as my high school students would say, things got real all of a sudden.

Before having our own children, the models for Jewish interfaith families I had seen were:

1. Kids who say they are both Christian and Jewish, but do not feel committed to either. When the going gets tough, I've seen kids jettison their Jewish identity.

2. Kids essentially raised as Christian, but who celebrate Jewish holidays with extended family and perhaps have a Chanukah bush.

3. A couple Jeff and I met when we were newly married: They had two sons, and they were raising one to be Jewish, beginning with his *bris*, and the other to be Christian, and this child was baptized.

In all three scenarios, the children are well loved, and there is no reason to believe that the children will be "damaged" by their parents' religious decisions. But I knew that these choices would not be comfortable ones for me.

I knew that it was important to me that my children be raised Jewish, with the added caveat of "no Christmas tree." But I could not articulate or even really know what it meant to raise my children Jewish in an interfaith relationship or how to do it.

At this point, we found out about Marion Usher's "Love and Religion" interfaith workshop at the DCJCC, and signed up. The other participants were all either dating or engaged. We were three years married, and I was five months pregnant. Clearly the other couples were taking a more organized and intentional journey than the one we were on, but it was helpful for us. It got us thinking and talking about things, and more importantly, it introduced us to the DCJCC and other interfaith couples. I think Jeff appreciated knowing that he was not the only partner in this situation.

Fast-forward: we had a boy, and three years later a girl, and we had no trouble finding a *mohel* who would do a *bris* that made all the grandparents feel included and a rabbi who conducted a naming ceremony that was clearly Jewish and inclusive.

The education and rearing of a child is when things started to matter for me. While I had only a little religious education, I had developed a strong Jewish identity, and this was what I wanted for my children. I felt that I couldn't control their personal idea of faith or their beliefs, or their choices as adults, but I did feel that I could shape their sense of personal identity, and I wanted that to include Jewishness. I didn't want them to feel like being Jewish was something they could put on and take off to suit the various moments of their lives. I wanted them to know that no matter where they were and whom they were with, they were Jewish, and I wanted that identity to be a positive and comforting one. If they chose a different path when they were adults, I didn't want their Jewishness to be something they could discard easily or thoughtlessly.

I still wasn't sure how to do this, and so I felt anxiety at various steps along the way. The stars seemed to align, though, and when it was time for our older child to go to preschool, the DCJCC was the most convenient for us, and it was a good fit. Our son (and later, our daughter) was getting exposed to Jewishness as a normal part of his life outside of home, and since the families at the DCJCC are a reflection of the neighborhood, we did not feel at all out of place as an interfaith family among the other parents.

When it was time to think about kindergarten, the director of the JCC mentioned the Jewish Primary Day School. I initially balked, because of our "interfaith-ness," but she told me that we would be perfectly welcome and not alone there. I spent the latter half of my childhood in a city that didn't even have a JCC, much less a Jewish day school, so I couldn't envision what it would be like. We visited the school, and we both really liked what we saw. I was apprehensive, though, as we made the decision to enroll our son. Was Jeff really on board? Was this going to push the envelope too far for him? Would we really fit in? Was I a "strong enough" Jew to carry the whole family through? This is something I wouldn't have felt if I were not in an interfaith marriage. But for all of my anxieties, I loved the idea of JPDS. Insecure as I was about my ability to raise Jewish children and create a Jewish home, sending them to a Jewish day school took that pressure off me, and it has resulted in an education for all of us. It has been a good fit for our family, and knowing that the children's Jewish identities were being reinforced outside of the home made me feel less territorial inside the home.

For us, DC has been a welcoming place. We have become a part of the Jewish community on our terms and in ways that are comfortable, yet at the same time completely unexpected. But that is the kind of journey we began thirteen years ago, without a map, without rules. All we had were our own backgrounds and personal ideas, and a commitment to each other, and then to our children. Nothing has turned out in a way we could have predicted. We have joined a Conservative congregation in the past year, although prior to that I never would have even imagined walking through the doors of a Conservative synagogue, interfaith marriage or not. But we had spent years trying out the various Reform congregations, and none of them felt right. Our affiliation with the JCC led us to JPDS, and at JPDS we met families who led us to the Adas Israel Congregation.

But because we are interfaith, the Jewish part of the story is only *part* of the story. Our children have a Jewish identity, but they also have a family identity, and that includes the fact that half of their family is Christian, including their father.

These are the choices we have made up to this point, and at every juncture so far we have felt welcome and able to find an acceptable comfort level. Other families will certainly make their own choices, and we hope that they have as positive an experience as we have.

*MARION'S POST SCRIPT
> When I attended their son's bar mitzvah at Adas Israel Congregation several years ago, I was moved to tears when Jeff stood on the *bimah* and blessed his son in Hebrew.

LISETTE

"I was raised Catholic, but…" followed by a shrug to show my ambivalence. I suppose my Jewish journey started with that offhand remark, made in 2007 in the atrium of my graduate program's building to a then acquaintance who also happened to be my future husband. He was inviting me to a Yom Kippur break-the-fast and a friend's birthday party later that evening, which I guess you could call a first date. Unbeknownst to me, I had given him the green light. Though I wasn't Jewish, I was what he would later call "religiously ambivalent," which was second best.

And religiously ambivalent I was. Allow me to back up a little bit so you have some context. My mother is a religious Catholic, and growing up we went to church every Sunday, church school, and CCD. I had a first communion, a confirmation, the whole bit. As a young child, I didn't really think much of this through. It was around the time of confirmation, ironically, that I began to seriously doubt the teachings of the religion in which I was being raised. It just so happened that that year coincided with world history in school, and reading and learning about the religions of the world, all practiced with their own certainty, fervor, and faith, made me doubt that Catholicism had all the right answers or that the Bible should be believed to the exclusion of other sacred texts.

By the time I went to college, some of my doubt had turned to something a bit darker. My later Catholic education seemed to be preoccupied with premarital sex, reproductive rights, and homosexuality, not the social justice focus that had been central to my mom's faith. What's more, I felt that the Catholic Church, in its harsh judgments about some social issues, had let my mom down in some of the most difficult moments of her life, like when a family member committed suicide (they did not want him buried in a Catholic cemetery) or when she and my father divorced (considered a sin). I thought religion should support people in their most difficult times, not make them feel worse, and I distanced myself further from Catholicism.

I enrolled in a religion course in my freshman year, wanting to explore other religions and find one that felt like a better fit. It was co-taught by three professors, scholars in Judaism, Christianity, and Islam, respectively. As an aside: I was shocked by some of the things that the Judaism professor said and wondered how he could say these things about not believing the stories of the Torah to be literally true and still be a deeply religious Jew. I chuckle at that in retrospect. At the time, though, none of those traditions felt like a good fit, and my enthusiasm for finding a new religion waned.

Even when I felt like I had rejected Catholicism, I maintained a sense that religion is an important component of a meaningful life. I was grateful to my mom for giving me a religious education, and I felt that it had been important in giving me a moral compass and a sense of duty for serving the poor and those in need. I wanted those sensibilities to be a part of my life and my future children's lives on a regular basis; I just wanted it to be through another religion.

Then came Jon. He made it clear from early on in our relationship that he not only wanted to raise a Jewish family in a Jewish household, but also that he wanted his spouse to be Jewish. Do you know how psychologists create these lists of stages of major life shifts? Well, I went through a series of stages kind of like that as we discussed what this would mean for our relationship and future family. During that time I sometimes felt like I was taking steps backwards, but in retrospect the stages look rather orderly and predictable.

- PHASE I   Naïve Interest (based solely on what Jon had told me about Judaism and no firsthand experience whatsoever) – Judaism is cool! I really like how it is an intellectual tradition that values doubt and questioning and does not profess to have all of the answers. It is cool that there is room under the Jewish umbrella for lots of different expressions of Judaism. I like how Judaism values deeds so highly as opposed to just thoughts and beliefs. Plus, I want to raise my kids in a religion.

- PHASE II   Resistance – I get why you want to raise the family Jewish, but why do you think it's OK to *make* me convert? Would you not marry me if I didn't? How come I'm not good enough as I am? Where is your half of this "compromise"?

- PHASE III   The Outsider – I listen to one Hebrew prayer at a casual Shabbat dinner. I think the whole thing seems weird, foreign. I visit synagogue and can't participate at all because I don't know the tune to the songs, let alone the language. I read the English translations to pass the time and get even more upset: I thought you told me that this wasn't all about God and blind faith—but that is actually what all of the prayers are about! I cry at services. All of a sudden Judaism doesn't seem so cool, and the idea that I have to do this to be with the man that I love feels like not a great set of options. I make secret plans to tell Jon I'm no longer willing to convert.

- PHASE IV   Learning More – I tell my fiancé not to join me at the Introduction to Judaism classes because I want to feel like I own this learning experience and that I can ask any ridiculous and out-of-left-field question I want without being embarrassed. The rabbi who teaches the course is a kind and patient teacher. She answers all of my questions deftly. I keep asking her what the rules are, because I am fixated on what I am *supposed* to do. She helps me understand Judaism in a new way. It's not about the rules; it's about the process. It's not about blind faith; it's about wrestling with the belief. She calms me down. As the course goes on, I feel more comfortable with the idea of conversion. Jon and I have lots of discussions about the "God stuff" as this is my biggest sticking point (more on this later).

- PHASE V   I Just Need Some Time to Let This Settle – Ideally the conversion was supposed to happen before the wedding. By the end of the Introduction to Judaism course, I feel much better about conversion. I can articulate what I think I gain from converting. I hang my certificate of completion on the fridge. But it feels rushed to convert in the few months before the wedding; I'm not all the way there yet on the inside. Jon probably secretly laments my earnestness, my sense that I cannot just go through the motions of conversion, but I want to feel that I own it fully. Rabbi Oleon, Jon, and I decide to take it slowly, so that when it happens, conversion can feel joyful and the timing can feel right to me. Rabbi Oleon and I meet from time to time. She assigns books for me to read, which I dutifully and excitedly order, but barely get past the first chapter of any of them due to a busy new job.

- PHASE VI   Acceptance – I feel ready. I start telling people I'm Jewish, even though I know there is an asterisk after that. A friend coins the term "ABM"—All But *Mikvah*-ed—to describe my Jewish status to fellow Jews. I broach the topic with Rabbi Oleon, my mentor. I am excited. I invite my family to a celebration. I am here!

The acceptance phase feels good. I like it when my family asks Jon a question about Judaism, and he looks to me to check that he answered right. I like it even better when I can correct him or remember a term first. I like it when Jon's family includes me as an insider in their discussions about Israeli politics. I like how Jon and I light candles, say three prayers, eat some delicious bread, and give each other a kiss on Friday nights. I like poking around the Internet looking at all of the Jewish social and service events happening in DC, even if I only ever make it to a few of them. I like looking at our *ketubah*, which says, "I will be your loving friend as you are mine." I like looking at the *mezuzah* I bought when we moved into our home. One day, I will like that so many life events will be marked in the same way in which they have by the Jewish people for thousands of years, and that I have a structure in which to celebrate, mourn, and take note of life's most emotional moments.

I still don't like the songs and prayers at temple (I do like the sermons), but they don't make me cry. In fact, it was at temple on Rosh Hashanah and Yom Kippur this year that I finally made peace with the "God stuff." To give you a little background, I consider myself on the less-believing side of agnostic. I don't believe in a human-like God. I don't believe that there is a God with a plan for my life or who answers prayers about my daily whereabouts. As a result, I struggled with this part of accepting a new religion a lot. My husband did. Not. Get. It. So many people who strongly identify as Jewish have similar feelings, or even define themselves as atheists, he said. It's no big deal, he said. Many other Jewish friends shrugged my concerns off as nothing to worry about. But I didn't see how one builds a Jewish identity without either cultural connection to Judaism (growing up Jewish) or some sort of belief in God.

In truth, a lot of that identity has been built as a result of doing Jewish things, but back to those High Holiday services.

I thought about how thousands of years ago, people were singing these same songs and saying these same prayers, and how comforting it must have been to believe that there was a God that loved them and cared about how they behaved, to stand together with their whole community, performing rituals and creating order in what must have been a scary, disorderly world. Maybe I don't believe in a personified God like they did. And maybe I don't read the Torah as a literal document as some of them must have. But I can still find a place for that role, a comforter of humanity in my life. I can find comfort in nature, in the rituals of religion, and in acts of service. I can find comfort in the genius idea that started with Judaism, that God wants humans to be good, and what that idea has meant for mankind ever since. I can find comfort in appreciating stories that are so beautiful and rich that Jewish scholars have not run out of things to say about them even after thousands of years. For me, this is an answer to the God question that makes sense right now. Sometime in the near future it might not make any sense, or my views about God may morph into something more traditional, but for now this is how I see it.

From our first conversations about conversion, I told Jon that my condition was that I feel I am gaining something from it. I have gained so much: a renewed connection to a religious life; a space, time, and rubric in which to think about creating a moral and spiritual life; a warm and welcoming community that is deeply committed to social justice; the comfort and peace that come with stopping and pausing to engage in ritual. As I look toward the future, I am most looking forward to what Rabbi Kirschner called "belonging as a beginner," which to me means figuring out ways to explore and expand my knowledge of the community in which I now belong. I am also excited about being able to affirmatively tell people that I am Jewish, that Jon and I have a Jewish household and a Jewish family. No asterisk!

My friends sometimes joke that my husband drags me kicking and screaming into adulthood. From getting married, to the decision to have children, to buying a house, he is always ready first, and I am always reluctant, dithering, overly cautious, and afraid of the unknown. Now that I am on the other side of all of these decisions, I can see so clearly that each one has enhanced and broadened my life in ways both expected and not. Converting to Judaism is no exception, and I look forward to discovering the ways in which it continues to enhance and broaden my life.

Chapter 1—Jewish Journeys

Marcia

Converting to Judaism? For the first twenty years of my life, I couldn't have imagined it.

I had been raised with Christian values, mostly through direct guidance from my parents, rather than exposure to their religious traditions. My brush with Methodist Sunday school when I was around five years old made me feel awkward and uncomfortable. Although my mom felt some religious education to be important, she didn't force me to keep going. And although my part-Sicilian dad was raised Catholic, it was not a positive experience, and he rejected the church as an adult. Our main interaction with Catholicism was driving my Italian grandmother to Mass when she came to visit. As I grew older, I developed a bit of skepticism of religious institutions and felt content keeping my distance. Instead, I found my sanctuary outside—walking in the woods or thinking on a beach. That was where I reflected and felt most connected with the world beyond myself. I was fine with that.

Then I met a charming Jewish man named Daryl. He was smart and funny, and he valued his Jewish heritage, traditions, and observance. This aspect of his life was important to him and who he was as a person, and the strength, comfort, and guidance this gave him made me take a second, more open-minded look. Through his eyes, I saw the values and the history, and I could see the inspiring ideas there. As we began to think about life together, Judaism would be a part of it. To be honest, I still struggled with how I could find my path there. But I decided the only way to know would be to learn about being Jewish. So I began conversion classes at Adas Israel Congregation, a Conservative synagogue in Washington, DC, under the guidance of Rabbi Avis Miller.

Daryl attended with me, as partners are encouraged to do, and many times it energized both of us when I learned something that he was just as excited to be re-learning. There were certainly challenges—I was a little intimidated by the Hebrew and all the details of Jewish observance. But there were also surprises—learning that questions about Jewish life and belief were not only accepted, but also encouraged. There was room for difference and doubt. Jewish life stressed *tzedakah* and individual responsibility. These things all felt natural and right. Despite the challenges and the change this amounted to, by the end of the class, I realized I could embrace it all. I became Jewish.

Becoming Jewish on paper, though, was just the first step. I wanted to feel more of a connection to this new people and culture. So I turned to something I'd always loved, something I could touch, smell, taste, and create—food. I began exploring Jewish food, especially the Ashkenazic versions we tend to associate with Jewish culture in the United States.

But in the midst of trying brisket and rugelach recipes—much to my surprise—my Italian heritage also seemed to call out to me to be revisited and explored. Growing up, I had had very little appreciation for Italian foods beyond the beloved greatest hits—meatballs, lasagna, cannoli—of my well-assimilated Italian side. As I explored Jewish food, suddenly it seemed a good time to also reach back and celebrate a part of myself that had been somewhat overlooked—to bring my past to bear on my present and future. Thus began a culinary journey to explore the foods of my inherited Italian heritage right alongside my adopted Jewish one.

Uniting these cultures and culinary traditions in the kitchen and at the table gave me a sense of wholeness and connection. I relished discovering the oft-intersecting history of these traditions over thousands of years as well as finding ways to make them uniquely my own. It occurred to me that recipes and stories like mine might inspire others trying to blend cultures and traditions in meaningful ways in their own lives, and that's how I came to compile and share them in my cookbook, *Meatballs and Matzah Balls: Recipes and Reflections from a Jewish and Italian Life*. Since then, I haven't stopped exploring and being enlightened by these culinary traditions and the stories behind them—and being delighted by what they all add to my Jewish life and understanding. It's been an incredible and illuminating personal journey.

And now I can't imagine not being on it.

JOHN

It was a powerful Jewish moment. Partly my Jewish moment. But mostly it belonged to my beautiful daughter Noa, who had become a bat mitzvah, in a celebration at which I gave a little speech in Hebrew on how much I loved her—*ech ani ohev otach*—and how proud I felt—*ani ge'e bach*. Now, standing at the edge of a dance floor, she had just invited my mom to step forward and light one of the thirteen candles with which Noa was honoring those who loved and had influenced her. Like my mom.

And as my mom, who is ninety-one, moved slowly toward her—three generations of us there—I felt a familiar pang of not being sure just how far I really want to go with this Jewish thing. Because, key fact, Noa is Jewish. But my mom is not. And I'm not either.

The Chosen People and Me:
A Chanukah–Christmas Story

1960, December. I flew home from kindergarten, clutching in my hand the first present I can ever remember making for my mom. It was gift-wrapped. It was a brand-new, unmarked 1961 calendar, commercially printed up, *but* glued by me, under the steady hand of my Jewish kindergarten teacher, Miss Lasky, onto a piece of blue construction paper, which I had also decorated with snowflakes that I had cut out of white paper.

Christmas was still a week away, but Miss Laskey had shared that this night was the first night of Chanukah, which I had never heard of, but she had told us that it was also a time for giving presents. So I burst into the kitchen…and thrust the present into my mom's hands. And she said: "John, this is lovely. Let's put this under the tree." And I said, "But Mommy, it's Chanukah!" And she said, "What?" And I said, "Happy Chanukah!" And she said, "But John, we're not Jewish."

And I said, "What's Jewish?"

Something landed in me as she began to explain how different people believe in different things. How our neighbors four houses away would celebrate Chanukah, but not Christmas, which struck me as terribly sad, but it also lit this spark in me—the beginning of a lifelong fascination with and attraction to the mysterious "Other." To voyage beyond the boundaries of the familiar. And it started with this simple thought: No Christmas? Who *are* these people?

A year goes by. And it's Christmas again. My parents gave me a twenty-volume encyclopedia set. And the first thing I looked up—verily under boughs of our Christmas tree—was the word "Jew." I read the entry. At the end it said, "Also see: Israel." I read that. Also see: Jerusalem. David. Psalms. Jericho. The Maccabees. Chanukah. Wow. It wasn't just about "no Christmas." These people had an entire alternate reality. *Star Trek* wasn't even on the air yet, and I was learning about strange new worlds.

A few years go by, and I'm about eleven now, and by chance a neighbor played for me a comedy record. It was a group of Borscht Belt comics doing songs and skits about the Jewish experience, and I just fell for this. I borrowed it and kept it for a year and played it and played it and played it. And I again looked up every reference and joke and piece of vocabulary. And this stuff got so deep into my head that I knew it by heart. Which I'm about to prove.

> *When you're in love…the whole world is Jewish…*
> *When you're love…the whole world is newish.*
> *You want to fly…you wink…and seem to feel so chipper.*
> *The moon is a yarmulke high in the sky…*
> *And each day is…Yom Kippur.*

That record was also where I learned that Jews only use the word "gentile" when they're talking to goys. Wow. They had a secret language. I was getting inside.

A certain day in high school was the last straw. I attended a Catholic boys high school, and one day for religion class we heard a talk from a rabbi about Judaism. And I asked a question, calling him, "Your Honor." He said, "You just call me rabbi." I said, "So how do your missionaries work when they go and try to convert people to Jewish?" He laughed and said, "We don't have missionaries. We don't try to convert. Really, we don't want you." Oh, God, I am so attracted to rejection. That was it. A club that did *not* want me as a member. Now I was in love.

So, naturally, I began dating Jewish women—from college on. They taught me much. Yiddish became part of my vocabulary. I opened the door for Elijah a bunch of times. Like an anthropologist, I mastered the many categories of Jews. Ashkenazi, Sephardic. Who knew? Reform, Conservative, Orthodox, Modern Orthodox, Reconstructionist, self-hating Jews? Bizarre phenomenon. Self-loving Jews? That I could relate to.

Look. It was obvious I was being called to an important crossroads. Conversion? No, I took things in a different direction. I married an Israeli. Which has worked out. Two kids. Great in-laws. The annual El Al flight to Tel Aviv. And look, I was inside my own Jewish household. Jews literally walking around in their underwear. Dinner parties where Jews unselfconsciously, in front of me, sat around talking about which movie actors were Jews. And the odd athlete here and there. Oh, the last Olympic Games! When it came out that gymnast, Aly Raisman, was Jewish, the emails flying across my wife's iPad on that! It was bigger than the Scarlett Johansson thing. Catholics don't do this.

Catholics do, however, have a different take on doing good. You try to do good as a Catholic, knowing that if you don't, you'll pay in the next life. But in Judaism, you try to do good because it's good to be good. Different. And I adopted that. You were really inside me now.

So why not convert? I don't feel Jewish. I think that's important. And there was this: by virtue of raising our kids Jewish—and I gladly embraced that; you know I'm such a fan of the Jews, of course I wanted to make two more of them—I became a minority in my own household. And I found the feelings complicated.

Like the day I picked up my son from Hebrew school, and he wore his *kippah* into the car. It gave me a jolt. Because I realized it was such a public emblem of his upbringing and mine diverging. Or the time my daughter was torn about having friends over from her day school because her dad's Christmas tree was still up. And she felt bad about feeling bad about it. I felt bad because I understood the clash myself.

Outnumbered, I had begun to want to hold on to my heritage. Which perhaps became the most Jewish thing about me.

So all this, it's a lot more complicated than listening to a record over and over again. But just as with that record, I do love the music, the nuances, the jokes, the ethics, the warmth of this community that has welcomed me to a Jewish life that I am not of, but that I am in the middle of. The way I figure it: let the record spin. I've hopped on, and I'm going along for the ride.

So when my daughter called my mom up to light the candle, her words to me from fifty-one years ago came back: "But John, we're not Jewish." Right. We're not. But my family is. Who are these people? Three of them are my son, my daughter, and my wife.

Chapter 1—Jewish Journeys

MICHAEL and MARIA

MARIA   Our Jewish story began on our second date. It was November 1990. We were at a bar not far from here, and Mike said the following:

"You're really cute. I like you. But two things: first, if we continue to date, and fall in love, and get married, and have children, the kids have to be Jewish. And second, if we have a girl, and if she's the first granddaughter of my mother or my aunt, she has to be named Sarah. Are you OK with those conditions?"

I said, "Sure." Why not? It seemed like a low-risk proposition, at the time. And he was cute.

So we did continue to date. And we did fall in love. And we did get married. And we did have a daughter, and we did name her Sarah.

It was not hard for me to agree with Mike's request because religion wasn't an important part of my life. I'm from Puerto Rico and from a Catholic family. I went to a Catholic girls school. My mom is a devout Catholic. Religion was a part of my life growing up, but I lost that connection as I entered adulthood and realized that I did not agree with many of the Church doctrines.

MIKE   But we didn't immediately execute on the Jewish thing. To be honest, I didn't know what it meant to be Jewish. My parents grew up in observant Jewish homes. But they were leftist, academic intellectuals who gave up religion pretty much as soon as they left their parents' homes. Growing up, we celebrated Passover and Chanukah, but never Shabbat. I didn't go to Hebrew school. I didn't have a bar mitzvah. I didn't know *aleph* from *bet*. Other than Woody Allen movies and Chinese food on Christmas, I didn't really know much about Judaism.
So how did we end up here?

MARIA   Well, I'm not exactly sure how we got here, but I can tell you how we got started: the Gan HaYeled. I was looking for a nursery school for Sarah, and a friend—a non-Jew with a background in early childhood education—was looking for a nursery school for her children. She chose the Gan, and I followed her lead.

MIKE   We started coming to the Gan functions. We came for Sarah's Shabbat. We came to the Friday night services that Robin Helzner and Rabbi Miller led. We came to Tot Shabbat. And we started coming to other synagogue functions. We attended Marion's interfaith workshop, where we met Jon and Ronit and others who are still friends today.

MARIA   And we started exploring what it meant to have Jewish kids. Which led me to inquire about converting the girls. By this time Sole had been born. Rabbi Wohlberg, our senior rabbi at the time, had a few questions for me, the non-Jewish spouse and mother, about how we were going to do it. And one of his questions was whether I had ever considered converting. The answer was simple. I had not. But I told him that I would give it some thought, and I registered for classes to learn more about Judaism in general.

MIKE   I never asked Maria to convert, but we did decide to take the girls into the *mikveh* and get them formally converted.

MARIA   And that's a great story. We picked a date, and we decided to celebrate the occasion with a little party at our apartment afterwards.

MIKE   But Sarah refused to go into the *mikveh*. I remember saying to Rabbi Wohlberg, "I'm just going to dunk her and get it over with." I'll never forget what he said, "We Jews don't do forced conversions." When we got back to the party and people asked how it went, we had to say that the mission wasn't entirely accomplished.

MARIA   The big turning point was our discovery of Friday night Shabbat dinner. Our friends began inviting us to join them. We reciprocated. It was like a party every Friday night. By then, I had completed three levels of biblical Hebrew and all of the Introduction to Judaism classes available, so I moved on to a conversion class. Totally non-committal at first, but by the end it just made sense to me. If my family was going to be an actively Jewish family, I wanted in…

MIKE   And then it just got totally out of control. Maria converted, and Sarah converted with her. And then, Rabbi Wohlberg asked Maria to be the "*mikveh* lady" here at Adas Israel congregation.

MARIA   I loved being the *mikveh* lady. It connected me with people at critical points in their lives—conversions of women, men and children, visits of brides and grooms, marking the end of an illness, and more. While I officially converted, in a way, Mike did, too. Because he really began from point zero. He was introduced to *aleph-bet* during my conversion class, which I had already learned. My conversion classmates were very confused at times—which one of the Sloans was actually converting?

When his father died in 2001, Mike came to *minyan* every day to say *kaddish*. Not long after that he began studying Talmud weekly with an old work colleague of his who is both brilliant and very patient. He became the *gabbai* at the *chavurah* here at Adas Israel and began daily study of *chassidut* with a client of his who lives in Crown Heights.

MIKE   Our Jewish life is very social. It includes this great group of families that gets together almost monthly to celebrate *kabbalat Shabbat* and dinner with lots of singing and eating and drinking.

MARIA   Yes, we call it our Friday Night *Chavurah*. The kids call it the *Chav*. We've celebrated new babies, b'nai mitzvahs, and soon our oldest kids will be heading out to college! We've also supported each other during losses. Some of our children have never experienced life without these families.

MIKE   And then there is Camp Ramah, where our girls have spent every summer since they were nine years old and consider it their home away from home.

MARIA   Yes, making sure our kids develop a strong Jewish identity has involved sending them to sleep away camp for eight weeks! We have to admit: it's something the whole family looks forward to! Camp has also inspired Mike to learn to play the guitar with the main objective being to lead camp-style Friday night Shabbat and *havdalah* services…a work in progress…

MIKE   Our family's Jewish identity doesn't feel like a work in progress anymore. It feels quite solidified by what seemed like a natural evolution. Not forced, but by making some deliberate, and some not-so-deliberate, choices along the way.

MARIA   That is not to say that things are always going smoothly. After all, most of Mike's family is very secular, and one of his brothers is raising Catholic kids. My entire family is Catholic, and some, like my mother, very observant.

MIKE   But we're working it out. Twenty-three years ago I told Maria that I wanted to have Jewish children, and I didn't know what that meant. Now I do.

ANDREW and TARA

Andrew's Story

Tara and I first met at Taco Night at the National Press Club, more than a decade ago, through mutual friends who also enjoyed the free tacos that came with cheap drinks. The two of us clicked immediately. While my Jewish identity has always been important to me, I wanted to ask out this beautiful, blonde woman even if it was probably clear that she wasn't Jewish. Despite growing up in a kosher household, and years of Jewish education, it didn't make sense to me at the time to limit my relationships to Jews.

We went on one extremely long first date—involving lunch, a monster truck jam with a coworker's young children, followed by dinner and a movie by ourselves. Several more dates followed, and we never grew tired of one another. I told Tara early on that Judaism was a big part of my background, and that if our relationship continued she should know that I would want to raise any future children in a Jewish home. Surprisingly—and thankfully—this didn't scare off Tara. We stayed together for several years, took classes on Judaism, attended "Love and Religion," and were married in a ceremony in 2013. Because the Conservative rabbis my family knew could not officiate at our ceremony, we relied on a friend from my hometown in Orlando to conduct the ceremony. It was effectively a Jewish ceremony—we signed a *ketubah* and pledged to adhere to the "law of Moses and Israel"—though Tara had not yet converted. That didn't happen until a few years later, after we'd had a daughter, joined a synagogue, and become comfortable with its community and religious leaders.

We overcame some big religious obstacles to get this far. When we were initially dating, my mother's first question when I told her about Tara was, "Is she Jewish?" I lied and told her Tara was half-Jewish. It seemed the best way to reduce the sting that would inevitably come from telling my mother the truth. I also didn't want to get into a fight over it while Tara, who was sitting across from me at dinner, was listening to our conversation.

It was always my intention to marry someone who was Jewish, not just my mother's long-stated wish. But over time it became more important that I have a relationship with someone I was genuinely in love with. Thankfully, Tara agreed to have a Jewish home and raise our kids as Jews, which in the end was what really mattered to me. If the classes we'd taken taught us anything, it was that it was best for children if there was a dominant religion in the house. When Tara agreed this would be Judaism, it didn't seem to matter as much that she didn't want to convert. I'd hoped that would eventually happen, but I wanted it to be her decision and not a precondition of marriage.

For my mother—who you can probably tell has always had an unduly large role in my relationship with Tara—it slowly became more important to have a grandchild than that Tara convert. At the same time, the Conservative movement is "squishy" when it comes to intermarriage: its rabbis won't conduct the wedding ceremony, but its synagogues will generally welcome you with open arms once you're married. In our case, this meant "converting" our daughter Eliana several months after she was born by dunking her in the *mikveh* and giving us the honor of a public naming ceremony one Shabbat morning. This made it easier for me to marry Tara without obsessing over her religious status. So when Tara decided to convert three years after we were married, I was thrilled, because it was fully her decision, and not a deal breaker for our relationship.

Tara's Story

I have taken a long path to my conversion, one I never would have started on if I hadn't met and married Andrew. We have been together for more than ten years now. He made it pretty clear at the beginning that he wanted me to convert, but I was not interested in Judaism, and especially not interested in Judaism for the sake of gaining his affections. This view was solidified about a year after we starting dating, when I met a good friend of his mother's who had converted. She gave me a piece of advice: don't convert for him to marry you, wait until you know he'd be with you either way. At that point, I had no interest in converting, or religion in general, but thought it was good advice. If I ever decided to convert, it would be my own choice, without the threat of a relationship ending.

After we had been dating for a few years, with the encouragement of a friend, we took Marion Usher's "Love and Religion" class. Although we saw a future together, we didn't yet know what it would look like. Learning from the workshop and our fellow classmates helped us create a path forward that we were both comfortable with. I realized that even if Andrew and I had our differences, they certainly were not insurmountable. Many of the couples in the class had overcome greater divisions, and alternatively, I could tell that a few probably wouldn't make it. The class helped to clarify many of theses issues though. Andrew and I agreed to have a Jewish home and raise our children Jewish, but I would not convert. It wasn't that hard for me to let go of having a Christian home, because outside of Christmas, it hadn't been a part of my life for a long time. After the class, I felt much more comfortable with where Andrew and I were at, and felt freer to begin to learn about and participate in Jewish rituals with Andrew. We visited family on Rosh Hashanah, and I even started to fast on Yom Kippur. I gladly participated in Passover Seders, and we started to go to Shabbat services and other activities at area synagogues and the Jewish Community Center.

After a few years, we became engaged. It was not a hard decision to have a Jewish wedding, even if we wouldn't be able to have any of the rabbis we knew well officiate. We were able to have a family friend officiate, which made the ceremony meaningful in a different way. Shortly after our marriage, we joined Adas Israel Congregation together and started to get more involved with synagogue life. Our daughter was born about two years after we were married. It wasn't until after she was born that I started to consider converting. First, we started coming to synagogue more frequently. We sort of fell into a Shabbat ritual, and I enjoyed it. And although Adas welcomed our interfaith family and me with open arms, I still didn't feel quite right about it. I was living a solely Jewish life by this point—only celebrating Jewish holidays (with the exception of visiting my family over Christmas), going only to synagogue, and I no longer considered myself a Christian. More importantly, I connected with the messages that the rabbis delivered in a way that I never knew was possible.

Tara's Decision to Convert

I really had never connected with Christianity. When I was fairly young, I had a conversation with my pastor's wife about where the Bible came from. She said the words came directly from God. When I pushed back, she scolded me and told me that this was something I should never question. I decided to fully walk away in the mid 2000s when those very words were being used to promote discrimination against entire groups of people. Most of the messages preached in the churches I attended never spoke to me, and I didn't connect with the theology.

I decided to convert for many reasons. Obviously, having Eliana changed my perspective on what it meant to have a Jewish home, and I want to be an active participant in her religious journey and to be able to help guide her. In addition, I've realized that having a source for moral guidance is important, and I connected with how rabbinical Judaism has interpreted (and continues to interpret) the texts in order to keep them relevant. Lastly, I've come to value the Jewish communities that I'm lucky enough to be a part of, both in Orlando and DC. Going to *shul* is a source of comfort—on good days and on bad days. There are always friendly faces, and it's a source of stability and guidance that I've come to appreciate so much.

Chapter 1—*Jewish Journeys*

BLANCHE and DANIEL

BLANCHE   I am Jewish by choice and converted five years after marrying my husband who is Jewish by birth. Daniel and I have been married for twelve years. We have two adult children from his first marriage and our ten year-old daughter, Daniela, who we are raising Jewish.

I was born in Peru, grew up in a Catholic family and went to Catholic school from kindergarten through high school. When I was 31, I met Daniel who also grew up in Peru, but who comes from a secular Jewish family.

We met in the summer of 2002 and started dating a year later after I moved to Washington from Austin following graduate school. I became interested in Judaism as a way of getting to know Daniel better. Daniel would tell me about traditions and Jewish holidays he liked to celebrate and the stories of his family's migration from Romania to Peru. I was struck by the fact that members of his family had been immigrants only a few decades before and that he had relatives killed in the Holocaust. The stories from history books and movies seemed real for the first time.

At the same time I had become disenchanted with Catholicism. The Church had become very conservative, especially in Peru, where a Catholic cardinal had been allied with an authoritarian regime that violated human rights. I never considered myself an atheist, and wanted to continue having a spiritual life, but no longer felt comfortable as a member of the Catholic Church.

That was the context in which we began our relationship. I did not practice Catholicism and Daniel did not attend synagogue. But he had a strong secular Jewish identity and a desire to show me his roots. Judaism was a topic we talked about, but never a condition for our relationship. It was a theme I explored in order to understand more about the generous person I loved and admired, who made me feel really loved for the first time in my life.

I learned about tikkun olam and the importance of repairing the world and the meaning of loving the stranger, not as a Christian "new commandment," but a pillar of Judaism. I learned about the importance of social justice and discussing rather than believing in dogmas. I learned that

Jewish identity could be linked to topics that transcended the religion: Humor as a cure for pain, for example and the millions of fiddlers on the roof. The more I learned, the more I recognized my own values in that tradition.

Judaism was there, accompanying us all the time in a secular way without us even noticing. Two years passed; Daniel and I married. We continued going to Jewish events, celebrating Pesach, attending services during the holidays, then I got pregnant and something happened—it catalyzed feelings already there. I was certain that I wanted my daughter to be Jewish, to receive Jewish values and to honor Daniel's family history.

We took Daniela to celebrate Shabbat every Friday at the Reform synagogue near our house. Sometimes we participated in the adult services after participating in the kids' service and attended services during High Holidays. We knew what we wanted for her, but didn't know what we wanted for ourselves. To understand and articulate what we were doing with our family, we decided to take an interfaith class at the DCJCC with Marion Usher. In class, we noticed we didn't have the dilemmas some couples had about religion. There was one religion at our home—Judaism. But something was missing. We didn't feel part of a congregation.

Marion recommended we attend a Rosh Hashanah service at Adas Israel, which non-members could attend. We went and were so taken by Rabbi Steinlauf's sermon we decided to try Adas Israel as our new congregation. We went to the Shabbat services on Saturday mornings for children led by Menuhah Peters and ended up in love with them. Menuhah was crucial in making us feel welcomed at Adas. After services we had conversations with her and other parents. Soon we felt part of something. I do not remember how, but we decided to convert Daniela to Judaism. Because I was not Jewish then, she needed to go through the conversion process. In doing so we passed a new threshold.

Because we thought it important for Daniela to receive an intense religious education, we decided to take her out of the day care center she was in and move her to the synagogue's pre-kindergarten, the Gan.

That's when I decided to take the conversion course, although I did not start with the intention of converting. I was lucky to have Rabbi Steinlauf accompany me on my journey and met with him every few months. I felt that I had found a religion in which I could practice the values I believed in. I converted to Judaism, becoming a Jew by choice.

My conversion was not easy for my parents, or for them to know Daniela was going to be raised Jewish, not celebrating Christmas. I did not try to explain my decision because I didn't want to start a debate. I didn't want to elaborate an untruthful narrative to avoid offending them. But I didn't want them to feel rejection about what they had given me as a child. I thought they needed time to learn more about Judaism and to accept a new religion in the family. So we decided not go to Lima for Christmas to avoid an uncomfortable situation, but I kept calling my parents to wish them a joyful celebration. Time passed; religion is not an issue in the family anymore. My parents have learned about and respect our traditions. They wish us happy Jewish holidays and we wish them happy Christian holidays. Daniela knows that her family includes Catholics, Jews, agnostics, and atheists and has grown up understanding that diversity enriches the world.

Now our family life is marked by the Jewish calendar. We celebrate the Jewish holidays at home and have a Sukkot party every year with pisco sours under the sukkah. Judaism has given us Shabbat, a weekly gift of peace for our family. It has filled us with joy and endearing friends. It and our synagogue has given us comfort in difficult times, filling us with security and a sense of community. It's a way for us to celebrate life in the middle of the desert, a way of transcending ourselves and feeling part of something bigger.

I cannot imagine my family in any other way than being Jewish. I cannot imagine myself not being Jewish. I feel deep in my heart that I have a very Jewish soul. Becoming a Jewish family was something that we built day by day, without any pressure from outside or from within our family—a journey about discovering the Judaism we already had inside.

DANIEL This is an unusual interfaith story. My father and mother were secular Jews. We never had religious celebrations at our home. When I was twelve years old, I surprised my parents by telling them I wanted to have a bar mitzvah. My father still says he doesn't know where that came from. That was the first of several "Jewish surprises" that have visited my family and me over the years.

I grew up in Peru, home to a very small community of Jewish immigrants, most of whom arrived after the U.S. imposed a quota on Eastern

European immigrants in the mid-1920s. My grandparents came from two small towns in Bessarabia (now Romania) and struggled to make a home in a new country. Though they spoke Spanish with a strong Yiddish accent, I don't remember them ever talking about Judaism, or about life—and much less death—in their native land. I did not attend the Jewish school in Lima, never set foot in a synagogue, and never had a Jewish girlfriend. The only Jewish memory from my early childhood was attending Passover celebrations, where my very commanding aunt exercised her powers as a Jewish mother for the extended family, gathering the larger family for a special dinner. We all wore kippot, the adult men wore tallit, we all sang loudly, and the kids had fun searching for the hidden matzo.

The second Jewish surprise was in my teens. When I turned sixteen, a conversation about birthday celebrations with my parents ended in plans for me to spend a gap year working on a kibbutz in Israel. That year was full of adventures, but I didn't learn anything about Judaism in my secular and socialist-leaning kibbutz. On the way back to Peru, I spent a few months working odd jobs in Paris. One evening I managed to get a black eye defending an Orthodox Jew harassed by a group of teenagers in the Paris metro. I felt I was identified as a Jew as well.

Many years later I surprised myself and my family again in honoring the tenth anniversary of my mother's passing by writing a book about Jewish life in Bessarabia and Peru, The Shofar and the Quena Flute. I was trying to understand my family history, but my Judaism was still very secular.

The biggest, most wonderful Jewish surprise happened years later. I married Blanche, who was not Jewish, but understood my yearning for Judaism even if I hadn't understood it myself. So when our daughter was born, we took her to Shabbat celebrations for babies and then for toddlers. When she turned two, we decided to convert her to Judaism and took her to the mikveh. A few months later, my wife decided to take a course in Judaism and started asking: Would I join her in taking these classes? Are we going to start attending services? Would I learn a bit of Torah and Jewish history?

Soon our daughter was attending the Gan; we were members of Adas Israel Congregation and we started celebrating Shabbat with friends. Blanche was so in love with Judaism she decided to convert. She has embraced Judaism deeply and has brought our daughter and me with her into this adventure as a family.

Though I still struggle with the religious part of being Jewish because of my secular background, the joke among my friends is that my interfaith marriage consists of Blanche helping me becoming more Jewish. I can't thank her enough for allowing us to celebrate life as a Jewish family.

TOMMY and SUSAN

The Courtship, the Marriage, the Children, and the Next Generation

I
The Courtship

TOMMY I was separated from my first wife for less than a year with joint custody of three children under the age of twelve and a demanding job on Capitol Hill. Meeting someone to develop a serious relationship was the last thing on my mind.

I was raised in a tight-knit Jewish community in Houston where attractive blond *shiksas* were admired from afar, considered eye candy and the source of teenage fantasy. In law school I married a Jewish woman from New Jersey, but who was non-practicing and not particularly interested in religious ritual or affiliation. Our three children had no formal religious exposure.

I had met Susan one time very briefly through work. It was after our second meeting when I decided to pursue a relationship with her. We liked traveling together and enjoyed hiking and running together, theater and art museums. She was a smart and ambitious lawyer, so we had professional interests in common. She encouraged and gave me an incentive to leave the Hill, join a prestigious law firm and begin to take my professional advancement seriously. Also, she was supportive of my need for separate time with and a continuing presence in the life of my children. In short, I adored her.

SUSAN I had an interesting relationship with Judaism all my life. When my mother was twenty-four years old, she had a romance in Havana with a Jewish doctor. At some point their relationship ended; he could not marry her because she was not Jewish. I wear a sapphire and diamond ring he gave her and have a jewelry box he bought for her while they were in Havana. The

Chapter 1—Jewish Journeys

box was always on her dresser, and she wore his ring until the day she died. She often said how much she loved him.

My parents met some years later, as World War II was coming to an end. They had four children and stayed together for twenty years in an unhappy marriage. Since my father was an executive, we lived in an upper-class neighborhood. Despite their difficult relationship, one of the few things they agreed upon was that religion and faith were important. We were affiliated with the Methodist Church; I attended Sunday school and church service every week, said prayers before bed, sang in the youth choir, and participated in Methodist Youth Fellowship activities.

The only other point of agreement between my parents was an intense focus on the importance of education and excellence. Both my education and music training involved Jewish teachers, who were highly valued by my parents and excelled in their fields. I was taught to respect them as individuals, and that being Jewish was a high calling. Many years later I learned that my paternal grandmother was Jewish, but it was a well-kept secret. That explained why I received chocolate gelt in my Christmas stocking. Until I was in the fourth grade, we also lived in a Jewish neighborhood, where many of my playmates were Jewish and exposed me to their holiday celebrations.

When I met Tommy I was attracted to his intellect, good looks, and character. I was terribly disappointed in the failure of my first marriage and yearned for a decent husband with whom I could build a warm and loving family. His being Jewish was not an issue for me. With our values about faith, family, and community being the same and even closer than we knew at the time, I was beginning to realize that Tommy might be the right person for me.

II
Married with Children

TOMMY   Susan has not converted. After we married, she insisted that we attend services. She persuaded—perhaps *cajoled* is the better word—my children from my first marriage to commit to bat and bar mitzvahs. Growing up in Houston, even having been "bar mitzvah-ed" and confirmed and having regularly attended a Reform synagogue, I was used to celebrating

Christmas in our Houston home, went to a YMCA summer camp, and even attended a private Episcopal high school. So in the early years, Susan and I celebrated a variation of Christmas and Easter, as well as all the major Jewish holidays. In fact, we celebrated almost any occasion in which Susan could cook a first-class dinner served in the dining room with my mother's china and silver and presents could be distributed to all the children.

Susan wanted us to have our own child early and my fourth child arrived the following August. Our daughter was a beauty from day one—like her sisters, but with blonde hair and blue eyes! (Remember, you need two recessive genes to obtain that result—my mother was a redhead with green eyes, so Susan's English genes found my mother's Polish ones.) Susan came up with a perfect idea and named our daughter my mother's maiden name—Daily.

At any rate, since our daughter's initials were DLS (Daily Lacey Susman), I called her "Daddy's Little *Shiksa*," but not for long. Susan decided we needed to have a permanent family temple affiliation and felt the most comfortable in a Conservative atmosphere, so we chose Adas Israel. Shortly afterward, Susan initiated the process of Daily's conversion at the *mikveh* and did enough research to be sure she had all the right signatures, so that Daily could marry an Israeli general if that was her choice. Again, Susan felt that the Gan at Adas Israel was the best preschool, and Daily could start her Jewish education early. Daily later studied and became a bat mitzvah, and her speech was about the origin of her Jewish namesake. She continued on through confirmation. Our life as a family was the life of a Jewish family.

SUSAN   Daily's naming ceremony was held in our home, conducted by Rabbi White, from Georgetown University (we attended his mixed-marriage group for several years early on) and an associate minister from Foundry Methodist Church, which I joined when I first came to Washington. I attended services there until Daily began her bat mitzvah studies. I did not want to send her conflicting messages at that point in her spiritual development. We also became more involved in Jewish holiday events at Adas Israel and participated in a retreat with Judy and Rabbi Wohlberg. I continued my faith journey at Adas. To this day, Rabbi Wohlberg's sermons are with me. His wisdom and scholarship were in the same tradition that I knew as a Methodist, always Old Testament/Torah first and then the stories and lessons to hold onto during the week.

A highlight of this period was visiting Israel—the first time for both of us—with Judy and Rabbi Wohlberg. This was a profound experience for Tommy and me. For many years, I attended Torah studies downtown with a group from Adas Israel.

Daily graduated from Yale, moved to New York, and continued her education with an MBA at Columbia, where she met her husband, who is Jewish. The story is he met her the first week at Columbia and was smitten with her. He was delighted to learn she was Jewish. He had not seriously dated any Jewish women before. His parents enthusiastically embraced Daily and they were impressed when she knew the significance of having an orange on the Seder plate! Rabbi Wohlberg presided at Daily's wedding, and I think he was almost as proud as we were!

III
The Next Generation

TOMMY Ours is now an empty nest, but it continues to be a Jewish one. My four children have wound up across the religious and geographic spectrum. My oldest daughter, Tara, married a Cuban, and while she still identifies and exposes her children to Jewish traditions (her oldest daughter is named Esther and loves going to her cousins' bar and bat mitzvahs), her household remains non-practicing. Susan is working on Esther. My second daughter, Shana, now Batsheva, married an Israeli and lives with her four children in a tight-knit *kabalah* community in Los Angeles.

The most remarkable turn of events involves my son, Micah, a committed nonbeliever who lives in Austin with his Catholic wife. Micah was the child most resistant to anything resembling a religious education. Yes, he had a bar mitzvah, but it was outside the traditional path and under substantial protest. But the birth of his daughter seemed to activate some ancient genetic trigger: he named her Helene after my mother, had her "*mikveh*-ed" at Barton Springs, and takes her to Tot Shabbat at a local synagogue.

Certainly I owe my Jewish heritage to my parents and ancestors. But the Jewish lives of my children and grandchildren bear the distinct influence of my non-Jewish wife.

SUSAN As for Daily, she lives on Central Park West in the same building in which her father-in-law was raised. Her first son, Roark David, was born hearing impaired, the result of recessive Ashkenazi genes that both Daily and her husband carry, but did not know about. Daily raised him as a hearing child and, by the grace of God, he can sing "Lucy in the Sky with Diamonds" on key. He is very handsome, looks like me, has Daily's sweet personality, but Tommy's irreverent sense of humor. He is now three and attends the Jewish day school his father did. Roark knows all the Jewish prayers, is a great athlete like is father, and adores his paternal grandfather, who usually walks with him to and from school. Roark attended camp at the Manhattan JCC where he also takes swim classes and has all of his birthday parties. Daily, her husband, Roark, and his new baby brother, Colson, are living a full Jewish life on the Upper West Side of New York using all the exceptional resources available to them.

HOWARD and SANDY

THE CONVERSATION AND THE OUTCOME
A Grandfather's Story

I had a terrible overreaction when my daughter first broke the news to me that she was in love with a non-Jewish man from a Catholic family. She had a bat mitzvah, was confirmed, attended Shabbat dinners in college, and took courses on Jewish topics. Our falling out over the relationship was so heated that we stopped speaking to one another for several years. I was devastated that the Jewish generational chain was about to be broken, and that I might have Catholic grandchildren. Thankfully, our relationship was not so damaged that it could not be repaired. Eventually, she married, and I participated in a beautiful wedding ceremony that included a *ketubah*, *chuppah*, and many Jewish traditions and Hebrew prayers. Almost all of the men in the bridal party and male guests wore *kippot*. Interfaith elements were also included, such as Christian Bible readings and a Catholic clergyman.

When my first grandchild was born, a girl, I was relieved to avoid the issue of whether to press immediately for a *brit milah* (ritual circumcision). Still, I had a lot of questions about how I could contribute to my grandchildren having a Jewish identity without setting off more fireworks with my daughter and son-in-law. After joining Adas Israel Congregation in Washington, DC, I learned about Marion Usher, a fellow member, who specialized in working with Jewish interfaith couples and families. She guided me back to a healthy and loving relationship with my daughter without compromising my strong Jewish identity. She helped me to understand that the best way to have a strong and loving relationship with my grandchildren is to have a strong and happy relationship with their parents, as well as with the rest of my family members.

Introducing Jewish customs into my grandchildren's lives can happen little by little over a long time—there is no rush. Instead of making demands, there are only quiet suggestions. The results to date have been very positive, but at a measured pace. My granddaughter has experienced Chanukah, *Pesach,* and Shabbat with toys appropriate to each. My granddaughter even wore a *kippah* at her first Seder. The marriage I once dreaded has turned out to be a blessing; my son-in-law is a wonderful husband and father. My family life is as happy as it has ever been. The road ahead looks bright—and it is looking east.

Sandy

NEW TRADITIONS FOR NEW FAMILIES
A Grandmother's Story

It occurred to me recently that my granddaughter, whose parents have an interfaith marriage, has had many more Jewish experiences in her toddler years than I did as a child, even though all of my relatives were Jewish. This is not what I expected. She celebrates many Jewish holidays, not just eating holiday foods, but also going to events and services geared to Jewish tots and young families. She listens attentively at Jewish story times and puppet shows. And when she sees Shabbat candles being lit, she runs to pull out her menorah so that she can participate.

How did this happen?

When I learned that my husband and I were going to be grandparents, I felt that it was very important for us to have a good relationship with his daughter, her husband, and our grandchild. I was very close to my grandparents when I was growing up, and I wanted to have that kind of relationship with my own grandchildren.

In addition, during the time between my daughter's engagement and wedding, I had read a number of books and articles about interfaith families. I was surprised to learn that many children of interfaith couples did not feel accepted in any religious community, felt pressured to choose between the religions of different family members, and often ended up feeling hurt and alienated. I was fully committed to making sure no one in my family ever felt this way!

Although my husband had gone through several tension-filled years and was very concerned about his daughter marrying a non-Jewish man, he also wanted to have a good relationship with his grandchildren. I am grateful that he was willing to listen to the expert advice of Dr. Marion Usher to help make that happen. She helped us develop strategies for approaching a variety of issues, such as Hebrew names, other Jewish and non-Jewish relatives, Jewish and Christian holidays, circumcision, Israel, and Jewish toys and books.

Discussing these issues ahead of time is extremely helpful. It allows us to go into different occasions with a plan or with several alternative approaches in mind. And if my husband and I have different views on a particular topic, we can air those differences in the safety of our meeting with Dr. Usher and work through them, instead of getting angry at one another because one of us blurts out something unexpected and perhaps inappropriate in front of others. For example, I know that no one will have a cow if there's a Christmas tree, and we can appropriately acknowledge attendance at a Seder or the lighting of Chanukah candles.

I think the most important messages we have heard are to be patient and to remain open-minded. We may be getting older, but our grandchildren are very young; they have all the time in the world to develop their own identities, Jewish and otherwise. And just as our parents practiced their religion differently than our grandparents, and we practice it differently than our parents, our kids and grandkids are going to form their own traditions. They are not going to be miniature versions of us, and that's OK. Being part of an interfaith family is allowing us to be part of new traditions, and I am confident that our grandchildren will have meaningful religious values and traditions in their lives. Being a Jewish grandmother is a wonderful thing.

*MARION'S POST SCRIPT:
> As I was leaving Rosh Hashanah services at Adas Israel Congregation recently, Howard, Sandy, Ian, and their precious granddaughter, Isabelle, greeted me. Sandy and Howard had the most beautiful smiles on their faces. Ian is their Catholic son-in-law who attended High Holiday services with his daughter, Isabelle, and his in-laws. Introductions were made, and Howard said, "This is the best High Holiday celebration that I've ever had; the gift of Ian, Alyssa, and Isabelle's being with us for the holiday and attending services."

> When I use the phrase "What's possible?" for grandparents to think about when they are dealing with their children who have intermarried, this anecdote serves as an example of an outcome that was totally unimaginable for Howard and Sandy when Alyssa and Ian got married.

1
SUMMARY

WHAT DO PERSONAL NARRATIVES TEACH?

The central theme underlying these stories has to do with your relationship itself. As a couple, when you can talk about difficult issues together and come to a resolution that affirms each of you, then decisions can be made. Taking the time to process these issues reaps enormous benefits. It can be hard, but listening attentively to your partner, responding empathically, revealing your feelings, and allowing yourself to be vulnerable forms the basis for good communication. As you co-create new solutions for yourselves, seek guidance where you feel you need it; you will expand new ways of being together.

Constructing your marriage is an ongoing process. Time brings new perspectives.

It is important to go with your gut, evaluate your decisions, and make time for fun and laughter.

2

WHAT IS A JEWISH IDENTITY?

In 1977, my husband and I moved from Montreal to Washington, DC. Did I automatically assume an American identity as I crossed the border? Did the Canadian part of me take a backseat to my new American identity? Would I still celebrate Victoria Day and eat Mackintosh Creamy Toffee? Or would I switch my allegiance to July 4th and other iconic American holidays like Thanksgiving and bake a pumpkin pie?

We all have a multitude of aspects that make up our identities: objective traits, how we see ourselves, and how others see us. What you choose to include or exclude contributes to how you decide to present yourself to others. Identity can be fixed or fluid and moves between the two positions.

How do we construct an identity? All of our experiences and our heritage add up to shape who we are. We pick some features and discard others. Over time, elements of identity change and can be arbitrary to our past images of ourselves. Identity can include aspects of our psychological, biological, sociological, race, gender, economic, and educational backgrounds, as well as political, religious, and national identifications.

Two people in the same family can incorporate an experience very differently, resulting in how we each see ourselves. When one parent was born in this country and the other elsewhere, how do both of these historical experiences get metabolized into the child's sense of self? Does one narrative become dominant for one sibling and not the other? Or perhaps the second child doesn't even incorporate the immigration story as part of his or her own narrative.

Identity is how we see ourselves. That can be different from how others see us and what identities are assigned to us. For example, Prince Harry of Great Britain is betrothed to a young woman who describes herself as an American actress. In truth, there are other aspects of her identity, which affect her professionally, romantically, internally, and in the public sphere. The media has revealed that she is divorced from a Jewish man and that her first name is Rachel. Her mother is African American and Jewish roots have been ascribed to her father by the press, a fact that has not been explicitly verified. Also, Meghan could very well have retained some 'Jewishness' from her former marriage, given that she was married in a Jewish wedding ceremony, not an interfaith one.

Why do we care to make an attribution onto someone we aren't personally acquainted with? By placing our heritage onto someone else, we imagine connecting with that person and affirming our own identities.

How do we express our religious identification? Is it a monolithic construction? Is it malleable? Does it have many parts? How do I express my Judaism? Is it the same, different, or somewhere in between from how I was raised? How much does religious practice describe my identity as a Jew? In what ways do my political views emerge from my Jewish values?
Do I try to lead an informed life based on the basic tenets of Judaism and do my Jewish values help me wrestle with decisions I make so that at the end of the day most of my internal parts are consistent with how I want my identity to be—a decent, empathic Jewish woman with human flaws?

How about my interests in theater, literature, art, music—am I being Jewish when I go to the Jewish Film Festival or attend a concert of Shostakovich's music or read a biography of Leonard Cohen? When I decide to try out a recipe from the famous Israeli-born chef Ottolenghi's cookbooks, am I executing my cooking identity, my Jewish identity, or both?

What does the identity of an interfaith family look like? Its members can see themselves in a variety of ways. If they decide to raise their children as Jews, generally the family as a whole adopts being Jewish as their identity. When a conversion has taken place, the family is automatically recognized as Jewish. Does the person who converts have a surgical excision of his or her past religion? Definitely not! They have their own extended family that they love and respect and with whom holidays and life-cycle events are celebrated. Here we see how the concept of "both–and" is an essential part of one's identity. After conversion, the person sees themselves with Judaism being dominant in their identity and their past religion present and receding. Both exist in different ascendancy.

When an interfaith family takes on a Jewish identity, it allows them to have a sense of belonging to a group. This goes in both directions. The greater Jewish community must take responsibility for including and incorporating interfaith families and allowing the families to experience what Judaism has to offer as a religion and as a caring community.

Some of the stories in this chapter talk about having a positive relation to Jewish identity. Others refer to the burden of difference. Along with difference can come elements of pride and defensiveness as in, "We Don't Celebrate St. Valentine's Day." The stories in this chapter illustrate the many possible ways that individuals and couples connect with their Jewish identity.

THE EXPANDING WORLD OF JEWISH IDENTITY

The Workmen's Circle commissioned a study about this subject and recently published its findings. It concluded that over one million Jews in the United States are actively seeking Jewish expression and engagement outside of synagogue life. To be more specific, one out of six Jews are seeking this identification in non-traditional ways, through cultural activities, spiritual practices, and the arts. They do not see it happening through synagogue affiliation.

This is a very important finding. When synagogues and Jewish communal institutions move outside of their buildings and meet the interfaith families where they are by way of creative programming, Judaism becomes more accessible, attachment to the Jewish community becomes possible, and the hope for Jewish continuity increases.

We need to do it better and more collaboratively. The focus is to help all people who want to have a Jewish identity.

When we think of innovative programming, we can imagine having Rosh Hashanah services in a nature preserve, Shabbat dinners held in non-traditional locations, afterschool Hebrew education held at the JCC, *havdalah* services carried out in the local playground, and facilitated discussion groups after an interfaith-themed film showing at a local Jewish film festival. In this way, people can be Jewish out in the community, meet others like themselves, and have multiple opportunities to explore and express their Jewish identity. How do we as a Jewish community show acceptance to those who are entering through these activities, for them to feel like they want to continue to be part of the Jewish community once they have had a positive initial experience? How do we actively prevent discrimination toward differing identities, particularly interfaith couples?

Let me describe two recent examples that model a "both–and" approach—fostering both inclusion and incorporation.

A few years ago, on Kol Nidre evening, as I was leaving my synagogue, Adas Israel, walking down the stairs and chatting with my friends, I looked out onto the front terrace and was delighted to see many young adults clustered around a semi-circle of chairs. I also saw drums, bongos, and other instruments in the center of the plaza. What was this all about? A few inquiries later, I was delighted to learn that two of the younger clergy members had offered a musical and experimental service, which they had publicized only though social media. It went viral! They had set up 300 chairs, but 500 people participated in this very meaningful and creative outdoor service in front of a very traditional synagogue. What an appealing and vibrant experience this was for all those who attended. Three years later, this service was held in a synagogue parking lot with 2,000 people and tickets were not required.

In Portland, Oregon, the Jewish Federation of Greater Portland funded a population study that produced puzzling results. They found that in the ten years since the completion of a prior survey, the Jewish population had greatly increased. The number was now much higher than expected. In examining the data, most of the increase proved attributable to interfaith couples and families—few of whom had any affiliation to traditional institutions within the Portland Jewish community.

In response to these findings, Federation officials created a series of "low-barrier and easy-entry" Shabbat services with dinner and prayers held during the summer at a local community pool. These were a great success. The outreach evenings attracted young families, mostly interfaith, providing just the right amount of "Jewish" for this population.

These are two examples that I see as creative and innovative. You might ask, "What's next?"

A welcoming community is crucial in affirming a couple's experience of building a religious identity together. Guidance and the examples of others can help them to make important decisions. Aside from feeling a connection to a larger network, there is an internal integration that progresses throughout this journey, where sensational and personal moments, creativity, and initiative foster a lasting connection with one's religion. For those brought up under a specific faith, these attachments are created over a lifetime of memories. As a couple makes its own joint choices as adults, initiative is pivotal in the cultivation of these experiences, which add to one's identity.

Along with institutional and community outreach, from a cultural perspective, including food, family memories, and local neighborhoods, we build ownership and feel more deeply aligned with our faith and practice.

Recently, my husband and I traveled to Montreal to celebrate our fiftieth McGill University reunions, mine from undergraduate college and his from medical school. It was wonderful seeing and catching up with classmates we haven't kept up with. However, this was not the highlight of the weekend for me. The most memorable experience was the tour of my grandmother's neighborhood, where all the Jewish immigrants had lived. Noah Richler, the son of Mordecai Richler, was the tour leader. Mordecai Richler is seen as the Phillip Roth of Canada.

There I was, standing in front of the tiny slip of a grocery store where my grandmother took me to buy Mello-Rolls, a cylinder of ice cream that you ate by ripping off the paper and pushing the ice cream up with the cardboard disc on the bottom. Of course, she spoke Yiddish to the shopkeeper. That was a given.

Next we walked on Esplanade Avenue, where my great-aunt and great-uncle had lived in the middle apartment of a triplex building. I was flooded with memories of Passover Seders held in that house. There were long tables, and my cousin Barry and I have wonderful memories of sitting at the far end of the table drinking too much Manischewitz wine, undetected by our parents.

The best part of the walk was going into the alleys. There I saw a replica of the back porch of my grandmother's apartment, where she used to hang the laundry; in winter, the clothes became stiff as boards from the cold. She had a wood stove and an electric oven, but she refused to give up her icebox, even while her new refrigerator stood in the living room. When my father finally threatened to send the appliance back to the store, she gave in.

So what does this have to do with my Jewish identity? Everything! As I walked on the streets, I could hear Yiddish spoken in my head, as I walked in front of the little grocery store, I could smell the challah breads that were baked in the back of the store, and as I walked on another street, I saw the old Jewish Public Library. This mélange of sights, smells, and memories are all part of my history and my Jewish identity.

While this is a narrative of a particular time and a particular place, this is what we need to create in real time now. Whether it is learning how to make latkes at the DCJCC, marching on the National Mall for fair wages, or attending a community council meeting to help fund affordable housing; all of these experiences create new memories about social justice, Jewish holidays, and building a Jewish identity.

TRANSMITTING VALUES THROUGH THE HOLIDAYS

Sometimes I wonder how anyone can have a simple thought these days. As my grandchildren like a story to begin, "A very, very long time ago," we would think and plan out how and what we were going to do for the holidays. We'd take our time, try out a few ideas, talk among the family, make a phone call or two, check things out with the extended family, and then draw a conclusion. In other words, make a decision and basically stick to it.

So how can we try to preserve some of this tried and true routine of families deciding about the holidays, given the web, smartphones, apps, and social media gurus who are out there bombarding us with advertisements and information to stimulate our brains to buy things we really don't even need? This is hard enough for anyone to manage. But then put on top of these demands the burdens an interfaith family has trying to make decisions about how to get through the holiday season intact and with some authenticity.

Here are some stories about families that focus on how they wanted to celebrate the holidays and took the time to make it happen. Both of these examples are about interfaith families who have decided to have Judaism as the lead religion in their homes. The stories elaborate on ways to honor the religion and parents of another religion in attending their celebrations. Both of these stories are about making meaning and building memories.

My friend Marsha, who is Jewish, has three sisters. Each of these women has many children, most of them in interfaith marriages. Some were married by rabbis, and others in non-religious ceremonies. The next generation of children identifies as Jewish and for the most part live in interfaith families, in which the parent of another faith has not converted.

It is the grandmothers, my friend Marsha and her sisters, who have assumed the primary responsibility for the transmission of Jewish identity to their grandchildren. Marsha does not miss an opportunity to teach her grandchildren about the basic tenets that inform our lives as Jews. As a member of the board of a local social welfare organization, she carefully explains to her grandchildren why she is on the board and what the organization does. She has involved them by bringing them to the facility where they can be involved at an appropriate level. She explains *tzedakah*, doing good deeds for others and charitable giving, by doing it. She uses a Jewish lens to explain her work.

Chanukah is upon us and Marsha connects with her sisters. On all Jewish holidays, they try to bring as many of the family members together as they can. This year it is twenty-six people including ten grandchildren. Marsha tells me that she is reluctant to let anyone else bring the food. This is how she expresses her love of family, and she is building a memory bank of Chanukahs for her grandchildren. She hopes and anticipates that they will associate Chanukah with her brisket and her potato latkes, originally her mother's recipes. In this case, the gifts are secondary to the food. Only the youngest of the children receive gifts, and only one each. The essential point is Marsha's clarity about her responsibility to transmit Jewish values and a Jewish identification to her grandchildren. She is doing this by gathering the extended family, celebrating a Jewish holiday together, making traditional foods for them to remember, and demonstrating the importance of Judaism and family using an ethical compass.

Here is a second story: Sally is a non-Jewish partner who attended my "Love and Religion: An Interfaith Workshop for Jews and Their Partners" with her fiancé. When I bumped into Sally several years later, the couple had married and now had a seven-year-old son. She told me that she was getting increasingly upset with the commercialism of Chanukah and wanted to try to make some changes in how the family approached the holiday. She saw the opportunity she had in front of her and sat down to discuss this with her husband and son. Together, they made the shift from consumerism to thoughtfulness.

After identifying some things they could do, such as volunteer at a shelter, cook dinner for another family, and other similar activities allowing them to show their generosity of spirit, they each voted and decided what they would do together to "show respect and honor to their elders." The family activity centered around talking and learning about this value as well as doing something to enact the true meaning of "Honor thy mother and thy father," one of the Ten Commandments. They baked brownies and delivered them to all four of the grandparents. The project expanded when their son decided they should include his aunts and uncles, and then he added the residents in the local nursing home. Sally's pride in what she had accomplished was visible in her smile.

Here is the central point: Do this as a joint process. Not all extended families live close by, and not all families want to be together. Try to talk about what is important in your life, and then together create your own ways in which you can do wonderful acts of kindness for your friends, relatives, and those in need. Engage your partner, your parents, and your children in this conversation. Share stories of past holiday celebrations and why they are memorable. In this way, you can create the opportunity to have a very different and meaningful experience.

WE DON'T CELEBRATE ST. VALENTINE'S DAY!

"We don't celebrate St. Valentine's Day." That's what my mother said. She would continue, "We are Jewish, and we definitely don't make a big deal about a holiday honoring a saint. Marion, you should know better."

I called my sister to check that I was remembering this correctly and wasn't making it up, and she said, "You know, you're right. Mommy never let us celebrate St. Valentine's Day." Granted, I was raised in Montreal, Quebec, where Catholicism reigned and where every Jew, most of whom were first-generation Canadians, was always on the lookout for any saint who might influence their children. As a result, I have vague memories at best of doing anything for St Valentine's Day. I think I once covered a box with red foil paper that I took to school, hoping to fill it with cards from my classmates. I remember sneaking the box back into the house through the basement door! If I told my tale to anyone today, I think they would chuckle.

Now I live in America with a husband, married children, and grandchildren. Here in the United States, even the name of the holiday has been changed from religious to secular. No one even thinks about the religious origins of the holiday. There were in fact three St. Valentines. While all three were martyred, the patron saint of the day was indeed a benevolent soul. During the third century when Claudius III, ruler of the Roman Empire, realized that unmarried young men made better soldiers, he forbade them to marry. It is Valentine who took the risk and performed the marriages clandestinely. He was celebrated for his acts of bravery and made a saint.

The romantic aspect came much later, at the end of the fifth century. The oldest valentine still in existence was a poem written in 1415 by Charles, Duke of Orleans, to his wife while he was imprisoned in the Tower of London following his capture at the Battle of Agincourt. In addition, February 14th is also the beginning of the birds' mating season in England and France, giving further romantic association with the day.

Given my work with interfaith couples, I realize that this topic has never come up as an issue for discussion. I don't think anyone thinks about the day as other than an opportunity to show love to another person.

So what do I want from my husband of fifty years? A gentle kiss and Leonard Cohen's new album, *Old Ideas*.

AN EVENING OF STORYTELLING ABOUT INTERFAITH FAMILIES AND THEIR JEWISH JOURNEYS

This storytelling modality can be easily replicated and is a wonderful way to transmit information to interfaith couples. Individuals and couples that choose to share their journeys publicly help their audience relate to the same conflicts they have faced. Both the storytellers and the audience join together through this medium and hopefully find mutual understanding.

A little known fact about Adas Israel Congregation is that there are over ninety families in our Conservative congregation who identify as interfaith. It is part of Adas Israel's mission to integrate this group into the many facets of synagogue life. On December 15, 2013, Adas Israel hosted its first storytelling event, which focused on interfaith families describing their Jewish journeys.

Ten people volunteered to present their narratives. Each of these couples was, at one time, composed of a Jewish partner and a partner of another faith. Some have converted, and others have not. All were raising their children as Jews. Nine of the couples had participated in my "Love and Religion" workshop, and one couple had been in the very first session I ran, in 1995.

Each person had five minutes to present his or her story, and what incredible stories they were! The themes ranged from "forbidden fruit" to how "conversions can make many generations of Jews" to "what you get when you mix an Irish Catholic with an Israeli Jew."

The audience laughed and sighed. Some stories were sad, some were happy, some focused on issues still unresolved, and some talked about how their children had taken on their own religious identity. All emphasized that it was constantly a work in progress. Each presenter spoke from the heart and allowed the audience an intimate view of their family.

For me, it was a very moving experience. I had presented this idea to Rabbi Holtzblatt more than a year previously and finally we were all sitting in the new Beit Midrash, listening to these astonishing stories.

GOING TO THE *MIKVEH* FOR CONVERSION
A Family Affair

Sonya has spent the last two years immersed in Judaism. Actually, her voyage started four years ago when she fell in love with Seth, a handsome Jewish lawyer. They met at a young singles event held at one of our museums. She had her dream job of junior curator of the exhibition; he was new to DC, having arrived for his first job out of law school. She was staff and supposed to introduce people to each other as well as take them on mini-tours of the exhibit. He was there because his law firm was one of the evening's sponsors. He also saw this as a golden opportunity to meet like-minded women.

After three mini-tours, Sonya realized that one handsome young man had followed along on all three tours. Finally, he turned to her, introduced himself, and offered to take her home when she finished work. And so it began.

Sonya grew up in a practicing Catholic home in the suburbs of DC and had a Catholic education. Seth came from an observant Jewish home, attended Jewish day schools, and, while he no longer kept a kosher lifestyle, he certainly saw himself living in a Jewish family and being attached to a Jewish community. He is a third-generation American with strong ties to Israel and the Jewish people.

The relationship became exclusive very quickly. Unlike many couples, they avoided the topic of religion. Both feared what the other would say.

After they celebrated their first year of dating, Seth spoke to the seriousness of their relationship and confessed that he hoped she saw that they could have a life together. It was Sonya who then bravely broached the topic. Yes, she did feel the same way, but wondered why they never really talked about their different religions. Seth talked about his fear of losing her, knowing she was a practicing Catholic. They were able to begin a conversation about their faiths, their religious upbringings, and their hopes for the future. Then they got stuck. Sonya couldn't understand why Judaism was so important to Seth, and Seth had a difficult time embracing Sonya's Catholicism.

With great courage, they decided to register for a workshop, "Love and Religion: A Workshop for Jews and Their Partners," at the DCJCC. Additionally, they sought out new ways to help themselves become empathic to each other's belief systems. They went to Shabbat services at various DC institutions and attended services at Sonya's church. They met each other's families and celebrated religious holidays with them. But for Seth, this was not enough. He was finally able to tell Sonya why he wanted to live in a Jewish family and have Jewish children. Sonya, after much back and forth, decided to convert and insisted that they would have a home based on a belief system. For her, if she were going to convert, their future family would have to be part of the Jewish community. Seth was surprised at her insistence and agreed.

In order to begin the conversion process, Sonya entered into a course of Jewish study, accompanied by Seth.

The culmination of this course of study, the actual conversion to Judaism, is a ceremony called a *mikveh*. Through this process, including an immersion into the pool of rainwater, Sonya became an official member of the Jewish community.

It is a very moving, spiritual, and sometimes awkward ritual. Sonya asked both mothers to be in attendance. While Sonya's mother really tried to understand her daughter's motivation to leave the Catholic religion, she ultimately struggled with it. She went on to say, "I am so upset, and I don't know what to think about all of this."

A *mikveh* guide is a person with an official role to act as a source of support and information to the person converting and to accompany family members throughout the ceremony. The main intervention for the *mikveh* guide is one of listening and empathy, putting themself in the other person's shoes. In this way, the other person feels heard and acknowledged.

The *mikveh* guide reached out, handed Sonya's mother a tissue, and said, "I see that this is very hard for you, and I want you to know that I understand how emotional it must be. While we often come prepared for such an event, we can underestimate our own reactions to what is happening. I want to tell you that your daughter will always be your daughter."

This conversation proved to be very important for Sonya's mother since it mirrored her reactions and helped her to accept her daughter's decision.

While there are descriptions and pamphlets available about this process, it is always much more personal for someone to help the family of another faith to understand the ritual. For example, this *mikveh* guide gifted the convert's mother a vial of water from the *mikveh*. For Sonya's mother, the gift of the water served as a parallel connection between the *mikveh* and her Catholic practices.

NOTE The *mikveh* guide is present as a helper for the convert during the process of entering the *mikveh*. She (or he, if a man is converting) is also there to be a support for the extended family. Often, when a woman converts, the mothers of both members of the couple are there to be supportive. Sometimes this is not the case. The ritual aspect is conducted by a group of three rabbis. One of these three rabbis, the sponsoring rabbi, acts as a pastoral role for the convert and her, or his, family.

Alienation and confusion can occur when we don't do enough to include the extended family by explaining these new rituals. This also includes the Jewish holidays and other rituals such as *brit milah*, bar and bat mitzvahs, and funerals. It is hard enough for the family of the convert to understand their child's new identity without feeling a sense of alienation. In our excitement to welcome the new convert, we need to welcome their family into the Jewish circle that the couple has created.

A PATH TOWARD CONVERSION

Are you seriously involved in an interfaith relationship? Are you pondering the idea of becoming a Jew by choice? Here are six tips to guide you as you go on this exciting journey towards conversion.

1. For the Jewish partner in the relationship, now is the time to express your gratitude and appreciation to your partner who is considering this life-altering decision. It is imperative that you demonstrate how thankful you are to be receiving this magnificent gift.

2. Sign up for an "Introduction to Judaism" class together. Not only will you learn, you will also meet other couples who are on a similar path.

3. Everyone who wants to convert needs a sponsoring rabbi to help guide his or her process. Before you pick someone, I recommend visiting several synagogues together. Research them and go to several services before you make an appointment with the rabbi. This will help you get a feel of the synagogue and congregation and decide if you feel welcomed there.

4. Go with your gut. Once you attend a synagogue where you feel welcomed and where members of the congregation have reached out, you have found the place for you! Book an appointment with the rabbi, and ask a lot of questions. If you still feel embraced after meeting one-on-one with the rabbi, sign up for conversion classes!

5. Talk to both sets of parents about what you are doing. Conversion is an important decision, and it is respectful to share this decision with your parents. The Jewish parents will be honored, and will hopefully share their appreciation that you are considering conversion. The parents of another faith need to be able to understand the conversion process. It is vital that they be reassured that their heritage will not be abandoned, and that they know that your future children, their future grandchildren, will be respectful of their traditions as well.

6. Celebrate this process. I recommend celebrating with a trip to Israel—how incredible would that be! If this is not possible, then take time to explore some Jewish museums in your own city. Here are some ideas of activities, organized by city:

NEW YORK, NEW YORK   Visit the Lower East Side Tenement Museum, Eat at Mile End Deli in Brooklyn or Russ and Daughters Café in the Jewish Museum on the Upper East Side.

PHILADELPHIA, PENNSYLVANIA   Visit the Jewish Genealogical Society of Greater Philadelphia or the National Museum of American Jewish History.

WASHINGTON, DC   Visit the United States Holocaust Memorial Museum, Sixth and I Historic Congregation, or the National Museum of American Jewish Military History.

MIAMI BEACH, FLORIDA   Visit the Holocaust Memorial Miami Beach or the Rubell Family Art Collection.

Mark the occasion by doing something that honors this momentous occasion.

GUGU'S JEWISH JOURNEY AND THURZA'S BABY NAMING
NEW AND RECLAIMED IDENTITIES

My husband was packing the car, and I was organizing the papers I wanted to take to the beach when the doorbell rang. I opened the door to find Gugu, my husband's cousin through marriage, standing there with a huge smile on her face.

"Wish me *mazel tov*," she exclaimed, "I became a Jew and an American this week!"

My husband comes from a large family from Milwaukee, Wisconsin. They were very different from mine, haute Reform Jews, well educated, many in number, and close as an extended family. Many of them have migrated to Washington, DC. We are so fortunate to all be reconnected. Time together is spent mostly around the Jewish holidays.

The latest addition, Josh and Gugu, arrived several years ago. We invited them to join us for the holidays, and they have been coming ever since. With each Jewish holiday that we celebrated together, I noticed Gugu's increased interest in Judaism. She began to attend local Shabbat services and started taking classes with Rabbi Shira Stutman. At this year's Seder, I noticed how knowledgeable Gugu had become; she asked questions, shared her curiosity about aspects of the narrative being told, and was a full participant in the Seder. In fact, she and Josh were the star performers at the table!

We were thrilled to hear that Gugu had decided to convert to Judaism and had entered her course of study with Rabbi Stutman. Her formal conversion at the *mikveh* in Adas Israel Congregation occurred a few years later. Three rabbis accompanied her, and she described the experience as meaningful and thrilling.

Gugu is a remarkable woman. She was born and raised in Zimbabwe and now is a lawyer in Washington, DC. When she married Josh, a Jewish man from an interfaith family, she did not shy away from Judaism—she embraced it! We are so delighted that Gugu has found Judaism, and we can't wait to celebrate many more Jewish holidays with her.

FAST-FORWARD THREE YEARS

I think one of the most joyful celebrations in Jewish life is the Jewish naming of a little girl. There is no pain, only sweetness and love.

Let's start from the beginning. Baby Thurza's father, Josh, is my husband's first cousin, once removed. My husband's maternal side of the family is fifth-generation Milwaukee Jews. They pride themselves on minimal ritual practice and maximum identity as assimilated Jews.

Josh was raised in an interfaith family. Somehow, our home in Washington, DC, became the gathering place for many of these cousins. How lucky are we? Another cousin who moved to Washington decades ago and whose husband is of another faith has given both her children a strong Jewish identity, a full Hebrew education, and bar and bat mitzvahs, and joins us in celebrating all the Jewish holidays. With great intention, she raised her children as practicing Jews.

Back to Josh, Gugu, and Thurza. As you can see, when Josh and Gugu arrived in Washington, it was only natural that they would gravitate to our family to celebrate the Jewish holidays. And so they did. The more Gugu came to the house, the more she wanted to know about Judaism. Through the guiding hand of Rabbi Shira Stutman, and a commitment to study, Gugu converted and established a Jewish home and family.

And this is how Thurza had her baby naming at our house. This magnificent baby was born in July, and three months later, surrounded by her loving family and friends, she was welcomed into the Jewish community.

Thurza means *delightful*. What a perfect name for this beautiful baby! May she grow in strength and become a major force in the Jewish community.

CREATING A JEWISH IDENTITY WITHIN AN INTERFAITH FAMILY
A Discussion on Effectiveness and Empowerment

A few months ago, Phyllis Katz of Kol Shalom Congregation in Rockville, Maryland, contacted me to see if I was interested in speaking at her synagogue. She had organized a series of discussions to better serve the needs of her fellow congregants who had grandchildren in interfaith marriages or interfaith parents in the congregation raising Jewish children, and she wanted me to conduct one of these sessions. When I asked who she thought would be in the audience, she said there might be both grandparents and parents. This intrigued me! I had conducted many workshops for each group, but this would be my first time having both in the same room. As I prepared some points to present, I also tried to get ready to dance on one foot since some of the issues that are relevant for one group are really not that important to the other. On the other hand, many are common to both, such as, "How do you transmit a Jewish identity to a child?"

As I looked around the room, I noticed that the grandparents sat on one side of the table, while the parents, some of whom are interfaith themselves, sat on the other. I took note. There was also a young couple there in a serious relationship, but not yet engaged. My task was to help these disparate groups to feel heard and acknowledged.

Rabbi Jonathan Maltzman welcomed everyone and told a story about one of the couples in the room. He had recently participated in the conversion of their two daughters. The girls' mother was of another faith, and the father had a Jewish mother who saw herself as totally secular and a Catholic father. They had gone to the *mikveh* at Adas Israel Congregation that week and were blessed on the *bimah* on *Shabbat HaGadol*, the Saturday before Passover. What a moving story! It was pretty hard to think of how to start my workshop after such a powerful vignette.

We ended up having an incredibly open and responsive group. Very quickly each person began to tell his or her story about what brought him or her to the group. Each story was more touching than the previous—from the Korean mother with a Jewish husband in the Foreign Service who had such a hard time finding a Jewish community for their family to an Israeli-born young woman married to a supportive man of another faith, but whose own Israeli mother never made Shabbat. As I talked with her, it became clear to her that practicing Shabbat was something she wanted to do. With the affirmation and support of the group, she decided that she would commit herself to making Shabbat for her family. People shared their struggles and how they found solutions.

The last person to speak told three short stories in which members of his extended family had flourished in their own interfaith marriages, all having chosen to raise their children Jewish. He went on to tell us that his own daughter was engaged to a person of another faith, and that he adored this young man and had already accepted him into the family. The father was delighted that he had found a rabbi to marry the couple.

Through these narratives, we see what a Jewish identity can look like. In addition, we witness the many possibilities that creative problem solving offers families as they forge a Jewish identity together.

THROUGH THE GENERATIONS
Mitzvah Day at Park Avenue Synagogue, New York

Several years ago, I had the privilege of watching my daughter lead close to 700 volunteers doing *hesed* (acts of kindness). We all talk about values, but it's another thing to get see your own child enact those core Jewish values. Congregants gathered to make sandwiches for the food pantry, fill backpacks for Ethiopian children settling in Israel, wrap toys for children of the JCC in Long Island whose houses were damaged by the hurricane, assemble Chanukah gift packages for house-bound seniors, and carry out many other worthy projects. As they completed one, they immediately started another.

Grandparents stood side by side with their grandchildren, guiding them through the tasks, which also offered them the opportunity to talk about the importance of what they were doing. I overheard a grandmother whisper to her grandson that he was doing such a good job assembling the package, and then she added how proud she was that he was doing something special for someone in need. While this lesson can be taught in the classroom, can there be a more palpable way to share with the next generation what really matters in life? This is transmitting values at its best!

As I watched my own grandchildren participate in these projects, I asked them what they thought about what they were doing. One replied that she was coloring a bear for a child who was sick; another was making a card for a package going to a soldier, and she told me it was important that we thank them for defending our country. The third granddaughter was overseeing a book project. She answered that she was doing this to make sure that all these books would be donated to a nursery school that desperately needed them for the children. Then she added, "And, of course, I needed to help out my mother!"

Being charitable is one of the three important tenets of Judaism. These pillars are *tefillah*, *teshuvah*, and *tzedakah*—studying, remembering what gives meaning to our lives, and doing acts of kindness. I was fortunate enough to observe my daughter, her husband, and their three children embody all three of these principles.

A CANADIAN LEARNS ABOUT AMERICAN THANKSGIVING
Understanding a New Culture and Creating New Traditions

My parents fly from Montreal, Quebec, to Washington, DC, to spend the long weekend with us. My father walks in the house carrying a small suitcase, which has a familiar smell. A smile crosses my face. My mother carries her own bag as she says, "Please be careful. The bag has all your favorite cookies, which I made for you and schlepped on the plane." It is 1977, Thanksgiving Day. Our friends are coming for dinner, and I have prepared food that I think is appropriate for the occasion.

We never celebrated Canadian Thanksgiving in Montreal. As observant Jews, my parents thought it was a great time of year to go to New York, visit our relatives, go to the theater, and have a great vacation. I have no traditional Thanksgiving memories to rely on.

Everyone is obsessing about where they will get their turkey, how they'll prepare it, how long they will cook it—the list is never ending. So I got it—you have to serve turkey. Then I remember my mother always served turkey on Erev Rosh Hashanah. I think of knishes, carrots, and green beans as the vegetables.

However, my father and I cook up another idea. He knows how much I love smoked turkey, a Montreal delicacy. The entire bird is smoked and covered in spices, with a heavy dose of garlic. He says he's willing to bring one down, along with the knishes and the *karnatzel*. *Karnatzel* is a thin, stick-like dried meat seasoned with fat, spices, and garlic—and it's delicious! I make sour coleslaw, baked beans with hot dogs, which we always ate with smoked turkey, and a pecan pie using a recipe from my days in Canada with maple syrup, a Quebec favorite.

As you can imagine, I totally miss the mark with this menu! My parents, my husband, and I, and even our friends, love this novel way of celebrating Thanksgiving. It is when I look over at my son and see his hangdog face that I realize what a disaster this was. He quietly mutters, "I'll never tell anyone what I ate this Thanksgiving!"

I'm a fast learner. In preparation for my next chance, all year long I clipped recipes. A month before Thanksgiving, I bought every magazine with a turkey on it. I obsessed about what was "authentic" American Thanksgiving food. The next year, the table had so many gourds, pumpkins, yellow and orange flowers, apples, nuts, and chocolate turkeys that there was not enough room for the plates. I created Thanksgiving on steroids.

After thirty-six years of living in the United States, we now have tailored our own favorite "American" Thanksgiving recipes. The pecan tart with maple syrup remains part of the menu—we need to honor and respect our Canadian heritage.

We can translate my experience of learning to adapt and incorporate new traditions to an interfaith couple making their first Passover or any other Jewish holiday where the traditional foods and recipes are handed down from one generation to the next. You can find many of my family's holiday recipes on my website, JewishInterfaithCouples.com, which can be used for those who have not inherited recipes and want to learn new ones. This is an opportunity to share everybody's culinary traditions.

A RANDOM ENCOUNTER AT BREAKFAST

Do we take a long walk, or do we go to the gym? The sun is shining, the snow is melting, and I already taste the perfectly poached egg at Open City Cafe, two-and-a-half miles from our house, which makes the walk perfect for today.

This is my hangout to meet friends for breakfast. This is Michael's first foray into Open City Café, although when he walks alone he usually goes to their sister restaurant, Tryst.

We see many families. It must be spring break, and they are laughing and having a great time on vacation. Next to us are a beautiful redheaded little boy and his parents. We start talking. They love Washington. They are from Dallas. They spent the week skiing at Massanutten, Virginia. I start laughing and recommend that they think about Vermont next year. They are such a sweet family. After much chitchat, I signal to Michael that we have to go home. He continues talking. I then say to them, "I have to get home and cook dinner for our Sabbath meal." She says, "Oh, my father is Jewish."

I'm hooked. I stay to hear her story.

Her mother grew up Protestant and was willing to raise their children Jewish. But in Dallas at the time, there were no programs for interfaith couples, and no welcoming clergy. For the baby naming, they went to an Orthodox synagogue, where her mother found herself in a separate women-only section, away from her baby and husband. She felt isolated, rejected, and dismissed.

As a result of this experience, this woman at Open City grew up with no religious observance. This is what she yearned for and felt that she was missing this important part of her identity. She decided to actively seek out a religious affiliation and sends her children to Christian school. Her Jewish father admires the education they are receiving, where values and ethics are the core of the curriculum.

Without any resources to help him, her father abandoned his religion, as did her mother. Her parents led a secular life, which left this young woman wanting.

Would the religious outcome of this extended family have been different if her interfaith parents had found support to create a religious life together? I would like to think so.

2

SUMMARY

Your identity is multifaceted and unique, as is every individual's. We perceive certain aspects of it as fixed, while others we either allow or determine to take new shapes as life circumstances and aspirations change.

I want to illuminate what we discovered in these stories about identity: that the influence of our internal structures of behavior, defense, and thought process, along with external variables of environment, family dynamics, and human connection, are part of a continuum. Part of sharing a partnership involves being open to learning, compromise, reflection, resilience, and possibilities, as we are active participants in our own evolution.

The impact of a negative traumatic experience can be deleterious for generations, while at the same time, we are strengthened by the positive effects when someone has a new experience, or even a new relationship with a past experience, that propels them onto a different path, one that they want and decide to embark on. The theme of courage flows through these vignettes and inspires new ways of reflecting on identity and building new aspects of that identity together with your partner.

3

THE WORKSHOPS: THE MAP AND THE PROCESS

For decades there were almost no resources for interfaith couples. It was a dark time in the contemporary history of the Jewish people. These couples were cast aside. At a conference at which I spoke, a woman in the audience revealed how she was married decades ago at City Hall with her parents crying, spilling shame over them as a couple. The trauma turned her away from Judaism.

The storyline continues to change dramatically for the better. Interfaith couples have a myriad of options where they can explore their dilemmas, meet couples like them, and find answers to their questions.

Couples who decide to seek resources for the health of their relationship choose to do so when they realize that they cannot solve their religious differences on their own. Some come when they are seriously dating; others are engaged or recently married. Other workshops are specifically for grandparents of grandchildren from interfaith marriages, while some programs are designed for parents with college-age children.

"Love and Religion" workshops are one modality that provide an environment in which couples can discuss how they will co-create a religious life for themselves and their children. Being affirmed by other like-minded couples in the group is an essential component of this model. Another value of these workshops is the emphasis on active listening. Empathy, standing in someone else's shoes, fosters understanding and transforms lives.

Honing of such a skill set can be gleaned from the workshop model by couples who are committed to mending the divide between their religious upbringings. Asking appropriate questions, revealing vulnerabilities, refining the ability to listen with attention and understanding, and making compromises are basic components to practice with each other.

These essays tell how couples and their families learn to share their values and reconcile their backgrounds and religions. Some stories demonstrate the importance of the Jewish community's response to interfaith couples and families. In the pieces focusing on "Love and Religion," you will see what a session looks like, whether it is for interfaith couples, interfaith couples raising their children in a Jewish home, or grandparents figuring out how to be involved with their grandchildren.

You will also read about innovative programs being offered in various cities. The most forward-looking and optimistic Jewish communities are building relevant programs, such as "Make Room for Latkes," a low-barrier event that draws interfaith and unaffiliated families toward Judaism. Many Jewish communities are now realizing that these types of Jewish experiences make affiliation available for interfaith families. My research has shown that if you build it, they will come.

SHOULD I ATTEND *Love and Religion: An Interfaith Workshop for Jews and Their Partners?*

Interfaith couples often ask me questions about what they should expect as they embark on their Jewish journey together. These are some of the questions that are most frequently asked. The topics shape an outline for an in-depth conversation between partners. While each couple is unique, they have one thing in common: they all want religion to be a part of their lives together.

1. How soon in a relationship do you broach the topic of an interfaith future with your significant other?

It is never too early to address religion, especially if your religion is important to you. Here is an example: A young Jewish man with a strong religious identity went on a date with a Christian woman, and found that he really liked her. Before their first date was over, he brought up his commitment to Judaism, raising his future children as Jews, and the possibility of his future spouse converting. I would agree that this could be seen as a bit of an extreme example. However, this young man had not discussed religion early enough in a previous relationship and was extremely disappointed by his girlfriend's reluctance to entertain the idea of raising their children as Jews. He was not going to make the same mistake twice, hence the rush to bring up the topic. He could not go forward unless he presented this essential aspect of his life to his date.

It is important to discuss religion early on in your relationship. In this way, each partner knows exactly what to expect from the other. Some couples choose not to address religion until they feel they are in a serious relationship. It is all right to wait, but I recommend that religion be discussed before couples decide to make a permanent commitment to each other.

2. What will we get out of coming to "Love and Religion: An Interfaith Workshop for Jews and Their Partners"?

You will meet other couples who like you, are looking for answers to similar questions. Each workshop session has a specific topic. I lead the discussion and then ask some questions for each of you to think about and answer. There is always plenty of time for each person to present his or her ideas, address concerns, and ask questions.

3. What can we expect to discuss at the "Love and Religion" workshop?

Topics addressed in the workshop include learning how to create a religious life together, how to talk to your parents about your relationship in a constructive way, and how to discuss what religion your children will practice. The issue of loss will also be discussed. You will both have to make religious compromises, and it is almost inevitable that one, if not both, of you will feel like you are losing aspects of your religion. The skills taught at my workshop will not only help you navigate religion, but they will also help strengthen your relationship.

4. What happens if we decide to raise our children in both of our religions?

Deciding how you want religion experienced in your home is a personal choice, and it is a choice that should not be made lightly. Some couples decide that raising their children in two religions is the right choice for them. Here are some resources that can help you if you choose to take this path: Interfaith Families Project of Greater Washington and the Dovetail Institute for Interfaith Family Resources.

My approach encourages couples to raise Jewish children. As a committed Jew, I feel my religion has much to offer for intellectual inquiry, basic human values, Jewish ritual, moral code, and a belief system that is essential to me. The core principles in Judaism of *tefillah*, *teshuvah*, and *tzedakah*—reflection, study, and acts of loving-kindness—inform my daily existence. My identification as a Jew makes me try to be a better person, a value I cherish.

Nothing about this decision is simple. If a family decides to raise their children in one faith, the child will be able to experience the other religion through their extended family. The extended family will be able to teach the child about their religion, even if a different religion is practiced in the child's home. It is my opinion that the child's religious identity will be stronger if only one religion is practiced in the home.

5. What should our wedding look like? How do we find an interfaith-friendly officiant?

Your wedding ceremony should reflect your personal and religious values, and it should also be respectful of those who are attending. It is important to have an open discussion with everyone involved about what aspects of each faith are going to be represented in the wedding ceremony. That way, everyone knows what to expect on the wedding day, and no one feels like his or her religion was left out. Getting married is a process whereby one professes his or her love and commitment to the other—this is the central component of every wedding ceremony, and it should remain the focus of your wedding day.

There are many Jewish clergy who will now perform interfaith weddings. If the Jewish partner or his or her family belong to a Reform congregation, chances are the rabbi will be available to marry you. An excellent resource is www.InterfaithFamily.com, which can help you to locate the appropriate clergy to perform the wedding ceremony.

6. How do we explain our decisions to our parents? How do we deal with their feelings about religion?

This is often the issue that takes the most time and effort. All parents want the best for their children, and sometimes they can miss the mark despite their good intentions. That goes for both parents and children. Take your time explaining your relationship to your parents. Meet with them in person if possible, and explain the seriousness of your commitment to each other, the concerns you have about your different religions, and the decisions you and your partner have already made. Depending on their reaction, you have many choices as to how to proceed. If they celebrate the love the two of you share and trust that you will be able to deal with the complicated issues that life brings, pop the champagne and celebrate.

Sometimes the conversation does not go as smoothly as you would like. It is important for you and your partner to anticipate what negative reactions you might get so you can be prepared for whatever the outcome of the conversation is. Supporting each other and being a team through this process is essential. Take one step at a time and try to answer your parents' concerns and questions thoughtfully. You can also tell them that you don't have all the answers and you are working on them together.

7. As an interfaith couple, will the Jewish community accept and include us?

It depends! Over the past twenty years, there is no question that the issue of outreach to intermarried couples and families is on every Jewish community's agenda. Recently, Washington, DC and New York City held conferences addressing this issue and called for the Jewish community to provide coordinated resources for interfaith couples.

However, keep in mind that not all communities are the same. You have to do your own research and make sure that the synagogue or temple you go to has as part of their mission statement a policy of welcoming and acceptance.

Locally, in the Washington, DC, area, we have websites such as gatherdc.org, and JConnect.org, which list all the activities going on in the Jewish community where interfaith couples would feel welcome. **InterfaithFamily.com** lists available resources for many cities throughout the United States as well as clergy available for interfaith weddings.

I hope these questions and answers have helped you to open up the conversation between yourselves and pursue further help with the discussion.

THROUGH THICK AND THIN:
"Love and Religion" Workshop

I am very excited that the JCC Manhattan decided to focus on outreach to interfaith couples, and I made a commitment to personally run "Love and Religion" for them. This meant going there once a week for four weeks. Certainly, this was not a hardship since three of my grandchildren live in New York!

The first session was well received, and I was very pleased. It took me a long time and many negotiations to convince this agency to do outreach programming for interfaith couples, and I have a vested interest in the success of the workshops so that the JCC Manhattan will continue to reach out to the many interfaith couples in their area.

Unfortunately, as I got ready to depart for the second session in New York, warnings about Hurricane Sandy were all over the news, with predictions of unimaginable damage on its way. The weather forecast was so ominous that I decided it was best to cancel the session. This was definitely the correct decision. Half of New York was affected with power outages and flooding.

Two weeks later, I was finally back in New York to run the next session of my workshop. I was feeling a bit anxious being there post-Sandy. I wondered if I would see the damage, if I could get around the city, and if it would affect the meetings that I had lined up. I also wondered if any of the couples were affected by the hurricane and whether they would come to class. I checked my email just before the class: one of the participants said she was on her way after a quick stop at Starbucks. Would I like anything? It was such a thoughtful gesture that warmed my heart. "Well," I thought, "at least one couple will be here tonight."

Everyone arrived. I was delighted. First, I wanted to check in and see how everyone had fared during the hurricane. One couple lost power and moved in with friends. One participant stayed in her office for four days. The third couple was fine. I decided we would extend the two remaining sessions by thirty minutes to make up for the canceled session. One of the interesting developments that emerged from the additional time was the opportunity to have a deeper discussion about the concerns each of the couples have about their religious lives. The safe environment of the group experience allowed each person to be open and revealing.

The central focus of this session was for each person to discuss their own religious background. Specifically, I asked the participants to think about how religion was transmitted in their families of origin, what parts they appreciated about what they had experienced, what they wanted to keep in the new families they were creating, and which parts they were no longer interested in retaining. The discussion was rich, interactive, supportive, and challenging. I was so moved by what they had to say and how empathic they were to each other.

One member of the group told us that he was having some concerns about whether the Jewish community would ever accept him or he would always feel like an outsider. He and his fiancée consulted with the rabbi who was going to marry them. The rabbi told him that he was a gift to Judaism. The rabbi also said that he made Judaism stronger because he was devoted to his Jewish soon-to-be wife and that he had committed to raise his children as Jews. This kind of affirmation by a rabbi allows interfaith couples to move toward Judaism.

Many New Yorkers demonstrated their strength to get through the storm, through thick or thin. In our group discussion, we navigated through some very difficult material. The same process of courage and empowerment served them both as they persevered through the storm and as they explored the dynamics of their relationships.

IS THIS REALLY THE LAST DANCE?
The Fourth Session of a "Love and Religion" Workshop

It's 6:05 p.m., and Virginia arrives first with her radiant smile and her open face, ready to begin. Three more participants arrive soon thereafter. Steven will join us as soon as he's spoken with the babysitter. One final member slips in a few minutes later, takes his seat, and joins a conversation that is already in full swing.

The atmosphere is electric. Beth's parents hosted an engagement party for her and Charles. One of the other couples in the workshop was also invited. All of us sit enraptured by this wonderful narrative, hearing how sensitive each set of parents had been to the other, as well as their efforts to share their backgrounds with respect and empathy.

Beth tells us how the Jewish parents carefully explained important Holocaust documents from their family to the future non-Jewish in-laws, how the non-Jewish mother had explored a Chanukah gift fair with the intention of buying items for her future daughter-in-law, and how much the families enjoyed each other. Beth and Charles are ecstatic about how well it went and how much fun they had that night. Charles, using his delightful sense of humor, teases Beth, saying that he knew all would go well. This rich discussion sets the tone for the entire session.

This concluding class focused on relationship models and how to have a healthy relationship. The participants were inquisitive about the dynamics that matter most and grappled with the malevolent concepts of contempt and defensiveness, as well as constructive relational techniques such as calming down, responding in an empathic way, and speaking non-defensively. The couples' level of engagement with the material allowed me to see how much they were learning and enjoying the workshop. They all wished the group would continue. They wanted to learn more about Judaism, and quickly embraced the idea of attending a "learners' Shabbat." They suggested classes on holiday celebrations, including latke preparation and cooking for Passover, a marriage workshop, alumni follow-up meetings, and a "hotline" for interfaith resources such as a list of clergy who perform interfaith marriages. All of these were excellent suggestions, and I am hoping they will be implemented at this particular JCC.

"LOVE AND RELIGION" WORKSHOP REUNION

This is the first time that I have done this type of reunion. This particular group wanted to meet again in a month. What an opportunity this presented for me! First, I could see whether they had coalesced as a group and had gotten together on their own. Second, I would have the opportunity to see what they had in mind for such a meeting. Third, I could answer any new questions that had come up since the workshop.

I was very excited to see the couples and to hear their news. While I had sent them all emails since the end of the workshop, I had only heard back from one person.

Everyone came except for one husband, who stayed home sick. We spent time together catching up. They were delighted to be together again. In this session, I saw myself as a resource rather than in charge of the session. Taking a backseat allowed them to bond together at a deeper level.

Since one of the couples was getting married two weeks later, everyone wanted to know more about the particulars. Specifically, they wanted information about the service, the clergy, the family dynamics, and how they had made their decisions.

At the end of the session, emails were exchanged again, and a desire to meet on their own socially was shared. Each couple expressed a wish to come together. They wanted to meet a few times a year. One person suggested getting together over Shabbat dinner. By encouraging them to pick a specific date, this suggestion turned from a "maybe" to a "definite."

This anecdote, for me, reflects these interfaith couples' desire to be part of a group of couples that is addressing similar issues and to have Judaism in their lives. As the Jewish community and synagogues and Jewish agencies in particular co-construct relevant experiences, interfaith couples can envision how they can relate to each other, to the greater Jewish community, and to being a Jewish family. Feeling welcomed and acknowledged is the precursor to inclusion.

AN ENLIGHTENED COMMUNITY CREATES NEW AND WELCOMING PROJECTS

There is nothing that brings a bigger smile to my face than a gurgling baby. So when Sarah and her adorable daughter came into my house last Monday, I was delighted to see them both. In a nanosecond, we were settled around my kitchen table, and the baby was cooing away and batting her precious little hand at the toy suspended from her carrying basket. What a wonderful way to start the week!

Sarah and I were meeting to see how we could do some programming together. The demographics of Washington, DC, are rapidly changing. Young Jewish, interfaith, and non-affiliated Jewish families are committed to living in the city, and more and more of them are using the facilities at our downtown JCC. As the director of community outreach to families, Sarah is interested in providing more services to these interfaith families. I was thrilled to hear this and to be a part of this endeavor.

Some more enlightened-thinking Jewish communities are developing a range of new and exciting ways to bring the unaffiliated and interfaith families to Judaism using new program models. They are relevant, local, and accessible. They all are affordable, if not free. For example, in Washington, we now have a series of "CityJews PopUp" events, including "Make Room for Latkes," "Make Room for Matzo," and "Havdalah Under the Stars." Similarly, in New York there is "Storahtelling" developed by Rabbi Lau-Lavie, which presents spiritual narratives with music and dramatization. The focus is to give these families a Jewish experience and to bring them into the greater Jewish community.

After Sarah and I reviewed many ideas and options, we settled on doing a hands-on project for families that included parents and children, a Jewish learning component, and a "take home" for both the parents and the children.

I love this kind of project, and I'm sure that this activity will be appealing to families that already use the DCJCC as well as to new families who have not yet stepped into the building. With that in mind, we brainstormed about all the social media available to us including the DC parent listservs, blogs, Google ads, our own DCJCC website (www.washingtondcjcc.org/families), my website, and many other web locations that could reach our target audience.

*MARION'S POST SCRIPT

We have been running this program yearly since 2013. We now have an effective collaboration between the Edlavitch DCJCC, PJ Library, InterfaithFamily, Jewish Food Experience, Love and Religion, Temple Sinai, and Adas Israel Congregation. Expanding our partners has always been one of our goals. We need all the significant communal anchors that hold the same values to coordinate this effort.

The program has grown exponentially, with over seventy people now participating in each gathering. Some have been before; others are new to both the JCC and to the program. Most live in the area, which represents a huge shift into the city by families that would have, in the past, moved to the suburbs when they began having children. This type of programming for urban Jews is extremely successful.

What do I mean by successful? In talking with most of the parents who attend, we learn that they are beginning to bring their children to the DCJCC to other programs with Jewish content, as well as recreational activities, and are inquiring about registration in the preschool. Some ask about the local congregations, and others want information about other Jewish community events. All these innovative programs have touched hundreds of interfaith families who were hidden in the past.

CUTTING-EDGE PROGRAMMING FOR INTERFAITH COUPLES WASHINGTON, DC CONFERENCE

On Sunday, April 28, 2013, the Jewish Federation of Greater Washington sponsored a conversation about interfaith relationships and families. This was a landmark occasion in which interfaith couples, Jewish communal workers, and donors came together to listen and to participate in a dialogue. The positive energy in the room was palpable. The audience heard presentations from interfaith couples, clergy, and both local and national groups. The breakout groups were buzzing.

Laura Mandel, from the New Center for Arts and Culture, showed a wonderful vignette from the play *Love, Interfaith, and Other Dirty Words*. A Jewish arts group in Boston, developed and is using this play as an outreach vehicle for interfaith couples and their families. The response was so positive that we hoped to present this in Washington.

The excitement of the day continued with three local rabbis participating in an honest and open discussion about interfaith families in congregational life. The audience was amazed by the creativity and commitment each one of the clergy members had to generating inclusion opportunities in their communities. They struggled with what was possible, and they all shared their dilemmas as well as the changes they'd personally made. Also on the panel was an interfaith couple who had just completed "Love and Religion: An Interfaith Workshop for Jews and Their Partners." They shared their desire to be incorporated into the Jewish community and focused their comments on wanting more than to be welcomed.

A community conversation facilitated at the end of the conference allowed for a rich dialogue to ensue between all the stakeholders, the interfaith couples, the presenters, and the donors. It was then that I was able to reflect back on this incredible experience we were involved in, especially listening to the two interfaith couples that presented their narratives.

Leigh and Jeff opened the conference sharing their story (see Chapter 1). They have been together for thirteen years and still consider themselves to be a "work in progress." Leigh's words characterized how little they knew when they started this voyage and how alone they felt. They eloped and got married in Florence because they didn't know how to navigate this complicated territory. Leigh compares the experience to exploring a foreign country without a road map. Their first foray into the organized Jewish community was when they took "Love and Religion" at the Washington DCJCC. Leigh was five months pregnant and felt they had to address the "religion issue," which they had been putting off. Having a Jewish identity was what Leigh knew she wanted for the children. How this would happen had to be charted. Step by step, both Leigh and Jeff associated themselves with the DCJCC, a Jewish day school where their children are students, and Adas Israel Congregation. This is a family that has become totally incorporated into our Jewish community, and we are privileged to have them in our midst.

Josh and Annie, the second couple on the afternoon panel, had just completed the "Love and Religion" workshop and begun their journey. Their first disappointment didn't come from the community, but rather from within the family: Josh's brother, a rabbi, refused to marry them. To the couple's credit, they were able to share their thoughts and feelings with him and move on to a better place, one where hurt feelings were acknowledged, and compromise was achieved.

Not only did my maternal feelings emerge as these two couples told their stories, but also my feelings of pride as I listened, with great respect, as these four people shared how they were defining their religious lives.

This was an exceptional day watching our community come together and explore complicated issues. I am grateful to be a part of this effort.

LOVE AND RELIGION
Workshop with Parents of Young Adults in Interfaith Relationships

It takes great courage to talk about your concerns in front of your peer group. This is exactly what this group of parents did one Sunday morning when we all met for "Love and Religion: Brunch and a Conversation." Most everyone in the group knew each other. They all had young adult children in college or of marriageable age. They came to discuss their concerns, especially how they could influence their children to marry Jewish partners.

Over the years, I have developed respect for the participants' willingness to be open and vulnerable in discussing this fraught issue. As people shared their stories, common themes emerged.

Almost every person present wanted to learn how to have "the conversation about choosing a Jewish partner" so that they, as parents, would be heard and could be helpful.

Some of their young adult children were already in long-term relationships with partners of another faith. While most of the parents didn't know how serious these relationships were, all of them agreed that they didn't want to alienate the partner of another faith. They wanted concrete suggestions as to how and when they should start this conversation about religion.

In reviewing our time together, the participants enjoyed hearing from each other and sharing their thoughts and feelings. For me, the goal was to have these parents feel more empowered to be proactive with their young adults.

Here are a few ideas to keep in mind if you are the parent of young adults:

1. It is your responsibility to transmit your beliefs and values to the next generation. You can choose to be an active participant in the process, or you can ignore this principle.

2. Every family has its own style of communicating. Clear and open is the most effective. It is never too early to share your thoughts, hopes, and dreams with your children.

3. Don't threaten your children. It doesn't work.

4. Celebrate Judaism. Be creative about Shabbat. Make your children's favorite recipes. Have them invite their friends, both Jewish and non-Jewish to your home for Shabbat dinner. Make your house the place to be for fun and meaning.

5. Share your own narratives with your young adults. Tell them about yourself growing up and include the stories, as you know them, from your parents and your grandparents. Take them to the city where you grew up, to the synagogue your family attended, the restaurants where you ate, and other places that were important to you.

6. Take the family to Israel. Nothing reinforces Jewish identity like a trip to Israel.

7. Be direct. If you want Jewish grandchildren, make sure that your young adult children hear it from you before they get married.

LOVE AND RELIGION
Workshop on Raising Young Jewish Children

It's not often that I get to do an entirely new program, but that is exactly what I did when I conducted a workshop for interfaith couples on how to raise their young children as Jews. Miriam Szubin, director of the Parenting Center of the Edlavitch DCJCC, and I had been trying to do this class for quite some time, but somehow it never got onto the schedule. Miriam is responsible for all programs related to parenting. Last August, she contacted me and was committed to making this happen.

Many things were interesting about the group of couples who attended this class. They were all interfaith, most had small children, one was pregnant, and another was preparing for when they had children of their own. None of them had their children in the JCC preschool. Most had been in the building before with their children, who had taken music, swimming, or gymnastics classes, or they had attended a holiday celebration as a family. All the couples except for one lived in this urban neighborhood. Five years ago, none of them would have been living in this recently gentrified neighborhood. Now we have many interfaith and Jewish families choosing to live, work, and raise their children in an urban environment.

These couples represent the "new Jewish family": interfaith, urban dwellers, hoping to use local public school and who definitely want Jewish experiences for their families, but not necessarily institutionally based Judaism.

Tonight they were coming to the JCC to learn how to raise their children Jewish. It was a privilege for me to work with these couples as they sought to find the path toward Judaism that was relevant for them. I am excited that the JCC saw its role as providing these experiences and bringing families toward Judaism.

It was my goal for the session to help these couples feel empowered as parents in their ability to raise Jewish children. These are the topics we addressed in the session:

1. JUDAISM AND THE HOME

   a. The essential place where Judaism is transmitted is the home. All basic values are passed along here. My family calls me the Shabbat Queen because I grew up in a home that celebrated Shabbat every Friday night, and my two children do it with their families as well. The celebration of Shabbat at home is the core experience for transmitting Judaism to the next generation.

   b. The Blue Box
   I like to give families a concrete example that they can immediately apply in their own homes. The Blue Box is the symbol of *tzedakah*. It is not only the money that you put in; it is the context. Here parents can tell stories about how their own families celebrated their values, such as helping the less fortunate, the homeless, and refugees.

   c. Celebrations of Jewish holidays in the home
   Here we talk about how the Jewish holidays can incorporate familial and traditional Jewish customs and rituals. It's an opportunity to experience the personal resonance of what Judaism has to offer.

   d. Food and family recipes
   Often, the person of another faith does not know how to prepare the foods associated with specific holidays. Sharing resources helps people feel welcome and informed.

2. CONTINUITY AND IDENTITY

   a. Couples can collaborate their ideas on how to pass on Jewish identity through exposure to religious practice, Jewish culture, theater, music, and art.

   b. As families, it is important to discuss the ethics and morals that guide your life—for example: "We do this because it is important for us to share and take care of others."

3. OPPORTUNITIES

a. Celebrate Shabbat dinner as a family. This is the keystone for incorporating Judaism into your lives.
b. Sign up for PJ Library books and activities.
c. Have out-of-town grandparents read to your children by Skype.
d. Light the Shabbat candles via Skype with grandparents.
e. Visit Jewish places in your city.
f. Make your own *Haggadah, mezuzah,* and so on.
g. Tell stories related to your family's Jewish history of immigration, childhood, education, and family relationships.

4. DIFFICULTY AND CONFLICT

a. Being in an interfaith family is not easy!
b. All religions must be acknowledged and respected.
c. Co-create your religious life together.
d. Look for help on the Internet: IFF.com, JewishInterfaithCouples.com.
e. Try out new Jewish experiences—for example, CityJews PopUp: Shabbat, different synagogues, and so on.

This type of workshop introduces these interfaith couples to the many paths toward Judaism and helps them to envision how this will be constructed in their own families.

LOVE AND RELIGION
Workshop on Intentional Grandparenting

Grandparents have traditionally been effective transmitters of religion within a family, and are essential in teaching their interfaith grandchildren about Judaism.

In creating a workshop specifically for grandparents with interfaith grandchildren, I envisioned an open forum where they could ask questions, share their concerns, explore new possibilities, and, most importantly, feel empowered about transmitting Judaism to their grandchildren.

Serving brunch first set the tone for this grandparenting workshop to be a welcoming experience for all in attendance. It was a very lively and diverse group of people. Some offered stories about their attempts to influence their grandchildren, and others shared that they felt they had already overstepped their boundaries. Those who attended had clear ideas as to what they wanted from the class and did not hesitate to participate.

Through a group-facilitated discussion, these grandparents were able to voice their concerns for their grandchildren. They talked about their hopes and their sense of loss. Within the group, they had the opportunity to talk through and learn how to create positive experiences for their grandchildren in learning about Judaism. The role of a grandparent is pivotal in the development of their grandchildren, and in this class, they learned the skills necessary to do "intentional" grandparenting. Having interfaith grandchildren can be a novel situation. This class helped grandparents feel affirmed, think positively, and learn how to impart Judaism to their grandchildren.

There was a wide spectrum of scenarios in their married children's homes concerning religious practice. In one extreme case, the Jewish parent was not very interested in being involved in Judaism. His mother, a Holocaust survivor, felt paralyzed in figuring out how to engage with her grandchildren without totally alienating her son. At the other end, a set of grandparents was already paying for a synagogue membership for their daughter and her non-Jewish husband. They also offered to pay for the grandchildren to attend the synagogue's nursery school. In the middle was another grandmother who was doing her best to introduce Judaism into her child's home so that the grandchild could grow up knowing about her heritage.

One of the concepts I had them consider was "What's possible?" Given a situation, how can they approach their children, be respectful of the non-Jewish spouse, and, at the same time, transmit their Judaism to their grandchildren? This idea helped them to think differently about dealing with the family dynamics. They also appreciated the concrete suggestions that they could implement. The group very much enjoyed this discussion. They felt a new sense of confidence in approaching their children and grandchildren.

There is a need in the community to offer support to grandparents of interfaith grandchildren. This group wants to explore their concerns and they want to learn useful skills for conversations with their adult children. All of them expressed an interest in meeting on a regular basis.

Here are some of the concrete steps that grandparents can consider as they explore the concept of "effective grandparenting" with their interfaith grandchildren:

1. Take risks.
   Talk to your children about coming for Shabbat dinner or the possibility of you bringing a Shabbat dinner to celebrate together in their home. I encouraged one set of grandparents to visualize that they could actually drive two hours to their son's home, bringing a prepared Shabbat dinner in their car. With great hesitancy, they approached the topic with their children. It went very well, and a new opportunity was created for these grandparents.

2. Make the Jewish holidays a time for celebration and education wherever you are, your home or theirs. Be purposeful. Think about your own memories of celebrating holidays when you were a child. Decide what you would like to replicate and what you want to change. Memories with Jewish content are critical to your family's history.

3. In your responsibility to hand down the family history, help your children and grandchildren become interested in family genealogy. You can use sites like www.myheritage.com and www.ancestry.com. This is

an excellent way to tell your story. A grandfather once reported to me that he was taking a memoir-writing course at the local independent bookstore. He added that he got his granddaughter involved by seeking her help with his computer. This was a win-win for sure.

4. While money issues can be complicated, if you can afford it, offering to pay for Jewish education and experiences, such as nursery school, JCC, Jewish camps, Hebrew school, and synagogue membership, can be seen as a great relief for your children. This can also be complicated territory if they think you are imposing on them. Test the water, tread carefully, and take baby steps.

5. "Do Jewish" locally, either in your city or theirs.
Seek experiences on "Mapping Jewish LA" on **www.Jewniverse.com**, or visit the Lower East Side Tenement Museum in New York. Most cities in the United States and Canada have museums, libraries, historical societies, and old Jewish neighborhoods that can be explored.

6. Visit Israel as a multi-generational family.
There is nothing more effective than taking the family on a trip together to Israel. Let them choose how they want to go. Your synagogue may have the perfect family trip, but that might not be the best way for them. Let them decide. Be grateful that you, as grandparents, get to see your grandchildren absorb this significant experience that will help shape their lives.

7. ABOVE ALL, BE PATIENT.

3

SUMMARY

The central theme of this chapter is to realize that the Jewish community offers various sources of help for individuals, couples, and families of intermarriage.

When you participate in a workshop or discussion group, you meet others who are trying to understand the similar issues you are facing. You learn new ways of managing complex matters, and you feel affirmed in your attempts to create solutions that work for you.

Within the workshop experience, there is room for you to observe your partner as well as the other couples. More voices add layers of diverse viewpoints and backgrounds, which lend clarity to the dilemmas being discussed. This type of facilitated group situation, in which one is meeting couples talking about similar concerns, creates an instant community, one that has a good chance of continuing on past the workshop. With communication comes strength and, hopefully, reassuring decisions.

4

FAMILY AND HOLIDAYS: CONFLICT OR RESOLUTION?

My mother had a saying, "Everyone carries a *peckel* [parcel/problem], and those who say they don't are lying." All families have dynamics and problems that they need to work on and solve. This is how families gain strength and resilience.

It is the responsibility of parents to hand down through the generations their family's history, religion, and ethical behavior. Being part of a family offers us a sense of belonging, a sense of security, and a hope that we will all take care of each other. These responsibilities are the ideal. We can be lulled into thinking that only our family has problems and other families do not.

The history of how Jewish families have dealt with interfaith marriages in the past is disappointing. Non-Jewish partners were ostracized. The Jewish partner was encouraged to break off the relationship. Another tactic was to force conversion prior to marriage making the marriage acceptable within the family and the greater Jewish community. Shame accompanied this entire process.

Up until the last few decades, when parents experienced interfaith marriages within their own families, they typically felt a sense of loss. Their hopes that their child would marry a Jew and continue the Jewish people vanished. Things have changed dramatically. Partners can more commonly discuss their religious conflicts openly with each other and their extended families. New possibilities exist where few did before. New resources such as InterfaithFamily, OneTable, and Honeymoon Israel have developed in response to the needs of interfaith couples. In many cities they can attend a "Love and Religion: An Interfaith Workshop for Jews and Their Partners" workshop, or learn how to make a Shabbat dinner, or go to a creative Havdalah service. In all of these experiences, they will meet other couples who are grappling with similar conflicts. It is up to the couples to decide how they will use these resources and structure their religious life.

Couples work within their relationships to determine the religious dynamic particular to them and their combined values and traditions. Parents and extended family add additional layers of complexity. Parents and grandparents have a tendency to project their hopes and dreams onto their children.

Holidays can be fraught with tension. They are often the place where family dynamics are acted out. You don't have to be an interfaith family to have that experience. Thanksgiving, for example, is always touted as the true American non-religion-based holiday, focusing on the arrival of the Pilgrims to America and our gratefulness for the harvest. Still, families argue over who is hosting, who is coming, how long will the guests stay, and more. Even without an interfaith component, there can still be family disagreements.

Add the complexities of an interfaith family and faith-based holidays and the atmosphere is ripe for squabbles. Which holidays will we celebrate as a nuclear family, and which do we celebrate with our extended families?

When holidays such as Passover and Easter or Christmas and Chanukah fall on the same day, it becomes particularly complex. "December Dilemma" has become a common phrase bantered about. For me, this phrase is overloaded with negativity. I prefer to use "Christmas and Chanukah: An Opportunity to Create New Family Experiences," which symbolizes a more positive approach to this quandary. It takes the burden off the calendar and places it on the family to sort out what will work and transmit this information to their extended families.

Holidays also present an important opportunity for transmitting core values to children, such as doing something for someone else, visiting those in need of company, and learning about cooperation as a family. Passing down family traditions of food, play, and rituals may not solve all the issues, but they certainly help to make important memories for everyone to cherish.

Many of the stories in this chapter discuss options and suggestions to think about as decisions are made. Holidays give families the opportunity to be together, pass on their heritage, have fun, and make memories. Clarity of mission and purpose enforces the process.

THINKING ABOUT ROSH HASHANAH

Is it time to think about Rosh Hashanah? Up until a few days ago, I would have said no. August is just coming to a close, and the Jewish New Year falls late in September, so why should I begin to focus on the holidays and introduce stress into my life during my calm, bucolic summer vacation in Vermont?

Three friends called recently and brought up the subject. The first was obsessing about the invitations she had received, deciding between where she wanted to go and where she felt obliged to go.

The second sent me the recipe for the fabulous bulgur salad she made for our book club last night, and when I called to thank her, both of us decided it would be a great dish for Rosh Hashanah lunch. So whether I liked it or not, the New Year was moving into my consciousness.

My third conversation, with another friend, centered on how and what we each think about as Rosh Hashanah approaches. She said this is the time when she focuses on doing something different during the year. This has been a goal of hers for many years. Sometimes she has something specific in mind; other times she waits to see what emerges. This conversation definitely resonated with me.

Allowing yourself to be courageous and try something you have never done before is extremely empowering. This summer, with the encouragement of a longtime friend, I bought a pink kayak. To be honest, pink was not my first choice, but it was on sale, and pink was the only color they had left. I have had more fun with my boat than I ever could have imagined. Last week, nine women caravanned to Lake Harvey in Northern Vermont and spent the day paddling, talking, eating, swimming, enjoying each other's company, and appreciating the experience.

In addition to focusing on what the New Year might bring for us, it is a time to contemplate what we can do for others and how we can make our spiritual life richer. Think about receiving love from your family, friends, and yourself. These Days of Awe create a space for introspection, evaluation, and renewal. This is the essence of the High Holiday experience for me.

IT'S EITHER TOO EARLY OR TOO LATE

"Everyone complains that the Rosh Hashanah holidays are too early or too late," my mother used to say. She worried that if the holidays were too early in September, it would be too hot because her synagogue was not air-conditioned, so everyone would complain, and no one would pay attention to the service. If the holidays fell in October, when the weather was wonderful and cool, she worried that many people would be annoyed that the New Year holidays would interfere with their travel plans to see the changing of the leaves in the Laurentian Mountains. In either case, my mother worried.

Well, this year was a true challenge. Rosh Hashanah started exactly two days after Labor Day. Families were just getting back from vacations, children were going to their first day at school, summer wasn't even over, and the holidays were upon us. I don't remember the holidays ever being this early.

What did this all mean for me personally? How was I going to make my usual Rosh Hashanah lunch, see all my patients in a day and a half, try to enjoy the preparations, make sure that I stayed "in the moment," find meaning in the holiday itself, and get pleasure from being surrounded by family and friends?

I started preparing for the holiday while I was on vacation. I sent out an email invitation to all those who usually come for lunch. This includes our children and grandchildren; our nieces, nephews, and their children; our cousins and their children; and our friends, especially those whose children are out of town. I love this holiday because it is all about celebrating the New Year and being grateful. Once I sent the email, I knew things were in gear.

The next step was to think about the menu. There are a few dishes that I always make. In fact, many of the people attending call me to make sure that I plan on making the dishes they adore. These include my gefilte fish and "fancy" macaroni and cheese. My lunch is always a combination of traditional dishes with some new recipes that look interesting. This year, because the holiday was so early in September, I decided to have lighter fare, more vegetables, and fewer desserts, namely, not five different kinds of cookies and squares. I didn't have the time to bake all those things, and no one needs that much sugar. My ice cream cake, blueberry tart, and Jane's delectable apricot squares would suffice.

Now follow along with my thinking; planning makes perfect, right? I knew I had many hours in the car as we drove home from vacation. How could I maximize this? Make lists, organize my time, focus on the tasks, corral my retired husband into doing errands and chauffeuring me while I was running in and out of the grocery stores, and, lastly, lure him into setting up the buffet table with me. Getting this far into the process already made me feel all would be manageable. The stress of the early timing of Rosh Hashanah seemed to be melting away!

This is what it all looked like: we arrived home on Sunday of Labor Day weekend at 3 p.m. By 6 p.m., the clothes were put away, and the mail was sorted and triaged, with nothing but important bills even looked at. Next we had dinner with our children and grandchildren and promptly fell into bed. We were so appreciative of our children serving us dinner and caring about us. It was an important part of this whole journey; it literally fuelled us in all ways.

It's Monday, Labor Day, and I move into high gear. The first grocery store run includes all the ingredients for the three items that I make and put in the freezer: the blueberry tart, the ice cream cake without the meringue, and the macaroni and cheese. With this completed, I have time to circle back and revisit the mail and the laundry.

Now it is Tuesday, and I take on my other life, go to my office, and see all my patients. The Rosh Hashanah preparations get put back into the recesses of my mind, and I focus on the issues at hand that I am presented with by my patients to think about with them. It is rewarding to be back in the office after my vacation. I enjoy working, sharing their experiences, their pain, and their joys.

After work, my husband, the chauffer, accompanies me on my next food shopping expedition. He listens to the radio while I run around the stores at top speed. There is one big problem—there is neither whitefish and nor pike for the gefilte fish. After a long discussion with the fishmonger at Whole Foods, I settle for turbot and cod. At home, I add a little salmon. It turns out to be a huge success, and I will continue to use that combination in the future.

Wednesday is upon us, and the holiday starts tonight. Surprisingly, I am calm. Somehow I decided that this was how I was going to be, and it was holding. Isn't there a saying that goes, "Mind over matter"?

I go to the office all morning. Luckily, my patients, some of whom are Jewish, decided to see me on Tuesday or were too busy themselves to come in. I am appreciative since I have all the rest of the food to prepare by 5:30 p.m. when I have to leave for our children's house. They have now begun to make dinner the evening Rosh Hashanah begins. How wonderful for us to reach this time in our lives. We are greeted by our two grandchildren, who are so excited about the holiday and grabbing our attention by singing all the Rosh Hashanah songs they learned and prepared for us.

Back to the cooking. I don't, for one minute, suggest that anyone reading this should try to make all these dishes in such a short time. I am someone with loads of energy and thankfully had my retired husband to help with the chopping, the prep work, and the groceries. Every dish I made seemed to have too many vegetables and herbs that needed to be chopped, minced, or sliced. At 5:30 p.m., all the food was ready for the lunch the next day. I brought a bottle of wine to my son's house. I think I drank most of it by myself.

In rereading this, I realize that I might have scared off anyone from making a Rosh Hashanah meal. I promise you it doesn't have to be this elaborate. It just has to be joyful. For me, one of the ways I express my love of my family and friends is through food, and what better time to do so than on a Jewish holiday.

THE DAY AFTER THANKSGIVING

The public media has now labeled the day after Thanksgiving "Black Friday," a day where you push and shove in the stores and end up buying a new flat screen TV that you really didn't need. Though our use of the term "Black Friday" emanates from taking retailers out of the red and into the black during financial crisis, from my experience, it could just as easily be in reference to the plague in England or the mood everyone is in after they come home with too many parcels, swollen feet, and a big headache. Or simply a term made up by some public relations firm to catch your attention.

It is this last phrase, "catch your attention," that I would like to focus on because for me the day after Thanksgiving begins the deluge of articles and workshops addressing the "December Dilemma." This is the catchall phrase for the issues interfaith couples have to deal with as they sort out their religious life together.

Yes, I want to "catch your attention" and open up this discussion with a different perspective. You can find many articles that talk about the issue of the Christmas tree and whether to have one in the house or not. Another thing you can read about is how to navigate the complexities of the extended families and how to accommodate everyone's requests. All of these discussions are very helpful and necessary.

However, here is another idea to consider and to explore. This time of year, with Chanukah and Christmas swiftly coming into view, can we spend some time with our spouses, our partners, and our children and talk about what we find truly meaningful during this season? This season offers the opportunity to transmit important values, ones that we use to create personal meaning in our lives.

Here is the central point: do this as a joint process. Talk about what is important in your life with your loved ones and together; create ways in which you can do wonderful acts of kindness for your friends, relatives, and those in need. Engage your partner, your parents, and your children in this conversation. Share stories of past holiday celebrations and why they are memorable.

Here is an example of how you can accomplish this. The non-Jewish spouse in a family told me the following story. She decided to sit down to talk with her two daughters and husband. She saw the opportunity she had in front of her. After identifying some things they could do—for example, volunteer at a shelter, cook and bring dinner for a family with a new baby, and some other activities that would allow them to show their generosity of spirit. They each voted and decided they would do something together to show respect and help people in need. The family activity grew out of their talking together and deciding how to enact *tikkun olam*, an important Jewish value of repairing the world. Together, they all decided to participate in the "Everything But The Turkey" event at their local JCC, where the community cooks and provides Thanksgiving food for those less fortunate.

This was an uplifting experience for everyone. It is the family conversation that created the opportunity to give a larger meaning to this holiday. Going shopping or showing compassion to others in need—you pick.

Remember, the day after Thanksgiving is always Friday, also known as Shabbat. Gather your family together, and welcome the Sabbath Queen.

4—*Family and Holidays: Conflict or Resolution?*

HONORING CHRISTMAS IN A JEWISH INTERFAITH FAMILY

The year 2013 was unique. Chanukah and Thanksgiving fell together, and we celebrated Thanksgiving on the second night of Chanukah. How did we honor both these wonderful holidays? Certainly, it conjured up all my culinary creativity. Should I make only sweet potato latkes? What about a sweet potato kugel? Brisket will really not do for Thanksgiving. My son suggested a turkey with seven extra legs attached so we could have a turkey menorah. Interesting recipes flew across the Internet helping people to acknowledge the traditions of these two distinctly different holidays.

It is usually Christmas and Chanukah that fall together, resulting in a multitude of challenges for interfaith families to work through. This comes up regularly in my "Love and Religion: An Interfaith Workshop for Jews and Their Partners" classes. The couples worry about offending their parents, they are concerned with what impact this will have on their children, and they express feelings of disappointment around the holiday season. There are many possible solutions. Each couple has to work out what is best for them. This is an opportunity for interfaith families raising their children as Jews to revere their grandparents of another faith and celebrate Christmas with them. The grandparents feel honored and included, while the Jewish interfaith family demonstrates respect for all their extended family members.

The following is an example of a different and more complicated situation. I recently completed two consultations, in which both families were struggling with a similar situation. The Jewish spouse in each couple had noticed that their non-Jewish partner appeared sad on Christmas Day. I was very taken with this observation as well as the sensitivity of the Jewish partner. They were at a loss as to how to fix the problem. Each couple had already decided to raise their children as Jews within a Jewish home. Neither spouse of another faith had converted. Neither family wanted to celebrate Christmas in their own homes. Going to the extended families was not a possibility. Relationships within their families of origin were complex and difficult to navigate.

Since celebrating Christmas with the extended family was not an option, we had to explore other solutions. The first family chose to travel with their children during the holiday season. The Jewish wife, who had consulted me, was both grateful that her spouse had made the commitment to raise their children Jewish, but also felt badly that Christmas was becoming an increasingly difficult day for him.

So we talked. I am someone who thinks that there is no one perfect answer. People have to explore many options. My favorite question to posit is "What's possible?" Having grown up in Montreal, Quebec, where the dominant religion was Catholic, I have vivid memories of the city being totally decked out for Christmas. In addition, my mother's birthday was on December 25th and I have many memories of eating in restaurants covered in grand seasonal ornamentation! These memories inspired my ideas as to how this family might make Christmas a better experience. I suggested that while they were travelling, they go to a restaurant on Christmas Day to have lunch or dinner. This was seen as a "win-win" solution. By eating out, they could honor their father's religion and background, and with the festivities at the restaurant, they also could better understand what their father was missing.

The second family, too, tried travelling during the Christmas holidays. While it worked once, with the arrival of a second child, a vacation during Christmastime became impractical. We had to come up with a more local option. Rather than just one solution, we created a few possibilities that the family could try out over the next few years. This is an important process for families to learn how to do: try out one idea, evaluate the outcome, and adjust the plans accordingly for the next year. In this case, one option was to consider going to the home of friend who celebrated Christmas and would be welcoming of this interfaith family. A second was to find a local restaurant that offered a Christmas dinner so that the spouse could enjoy their heritage.

Follow-up phone calls informed me that both Jewish spouses felt so relieved about having found ways to help their partners feel better, to honor their religion, and to teach their children about mutual respect.

SURROUNDED BY THE MAGIC OF CHRISTMAS, CAN WE MAKE CHANUKAH MEMORABLE?

I had forgotten what it was like to be in New York City the week after Thanksgiving. The streets and sidewalks are jammed with people. The buses, filled with families from the surrounding areas, disgorge all their occupants at Rockefeller Center to see the famous tree, the exciting Christmas windows across the street at Saks Fifth Avenue, and a myriad of other lush displays. All I could think of as I was in the midst of this frenzy was the interfaith couples I have worked with and the concerns they have to manage.

Putting aside the throngs of people, which presents its own problem, there is no question that the Rockefeller tree is totally magical. In fact, it is irresistible, and I found myself struggling to get a clear view so I, too, could take a picture of the entire scene.

Despite the fact that we Jews are a small minority within a country that claims separation of a church and state, the dominant religious theme is clearly Christian. Putting up a big menorah in the middle of the town square just doesn't compete!

What to do as a Jew to make memories? Create traditions. Throw a party, tell the account of Chanukah through storytelling, or make up a play. Invite your friends and family over, and introduce a new holiday to those of other faiths. Create a new Chanukah cocktail, play games with Chanukah gelt, and exchange outrageous gifts with each other.

I grew up using only one menorah (*chanukiah*). We have now changed this ritual to include the lighting of many menorahs, which, when lit together, radiate their own kind of magic.

Since I love to cook, and people seem to enjoy my food, I always have people over for dinner and to light the menorahs. You can find two of my favorite recipes for a typical Ashkenazi Chanukah meal of brisket and latkes on my website, JewishInterfaithCouples.com.

The stark contrast between the commercialism and availability of Christmas spirit and lavish décor and the home-based celebration of Chanukah can leave us feeling somewhat envious. However, with the celebration of Chanukah, we have a profound opportunity to build personal connections to our own holiday traditions, to tell the story, and to bring families together year after year.

ACTUALLY, SANTA IS JEWISH!

Who would have ever thought that we would take our grandchildren, Tess and Joseph, to see Santa? There we were having just finished lunch at their favorite restaurant when my husband and I had a yearning for a cappuccino. Off we go to the coffee stand located in the lobby of the Mazza Gallery. It was Nana who spotted Santa, and we all went over to see what was happening. A Toy Soldier was walking around on stilts, and Santa Claus was sitting on his throne. The photographer was set up for families to get their perfect picture for their Christmas cards. So I said, "Why not? Let's all go and talk to Santa."

Up we marched to meet Santa. I introduced Joseph and Tess to him, saying, "Santa, these are my grandchildren, Tess and Joseph. They are Jewish, and I have told them that Santa brings joy and happiness to all the people of the world." Without skipping a beat, Santa replies, "It's so nice to meet you. My name is Marty, and I am Jewish!" He continued, "Your grandmother is correct—Santa gives out *tzedakah* to all the people of the world," at which point Tess pipes up and tells us all, "I know what *tzedakah* means. I learned about it when I went to [Temple Sinai's] nursery school." She proceeded to inform us all saying, "*Tzedakah* is when you give money to poor people."

So, you see, Santa really is Jewish.

CHRISTMAS IN VERMONT

Every year, on the eve of December 24th, twenty-nine Jews and three Catholics meet in Waterbury Center, Vermont, and have a party. You might think it is to celebrate the birth of Christ. It is not. What we celebrate is the annual reunion of the Lazar family, a big Jewish clan, the core of whom live in Montreal, with others scattered throughout the Northeast. What is this reunion all about? It is about changing the past. This is a family that had been fractured. In the generation before us, the siblings didn't talk to each other for years. Some repairs have been made, but not enough. I remember that a cousin, whom I had met once several years prior in California, was in Washington, and the first question he asked me was if I knew why the "Montrealers" had ostracized his mother. Like in most families where secrets are kept hidden for generations, I had no idea how or why this had happened. By the end of the evening, we decided we could try and make it different for the next generation, our children.

I can't even recall how our Christmas Eve Vermont tradition actually started. Was it my cousin, Susan, who realized that both my sister and I were all in our Vermont houses during the Christmas holidays, or was it I who invited myself to share in Susan's family's celebration of Christmas? The word had already spread in the family that it was quite an event. She had married a wonderful man of another faith. Susan and Ricki, a Catholic widower with two young boys, celebrated both the Jewish and Christian holidays. Her in-laws sent a mountain of presents, the tree was splendiferous, and everybody had a wonderful time. My sister and I longed to be included. Plus, Susan and Ricki now had two little girls of their own, and we wanted to get to know our new cousins.

Can anything compete with Christmas? No. One year, when I was a little girl, I remember putting up one of my icky brown, ribbed, long stockings on the fireplace flue knob. My mother understood what I was doing and put an orange in my stocking. I thought that was just fabulous. My father, on the other hand, had a fit. He took his Judaism very seriously and was outraged by my behavior, which he thought was sacrilegious. Actually, he never knew that my mother allowed our housekeeper to have a miniature tree in her bedroom. You know, one of those two-feet-high, plastic things. No matter how little it was, I thought it was pure magic.

So there we are, the Lazar clan, going through the rituals of the evening. Barry, Susan's brother, always makes *papadum* bread; Jean, Susan's father's wife, does the lamb stew; and Marge, Susan's mother, a secular Jew, cooks the ham according to her family recipe. Many other dishes come to the table, and careful attention is paid to everyone's food restrictions. While no one in the family keeps kosher anymore, some are now vegetarians, a sign of the times.

We eat, we drink, we laugh, we reminisce, and we make fun of each other. We fight about politics. We share books that we have read and loved. We discover new truths, and we always toast Susan and Ricki for putting up with us year after year after year. Actually, one time they had to put all of us up overnight. During the evening, the soft snow falling turned to rain, the temperature dropped to ten degrees below zero, and the roads were covered with black ice. We all slept over, some in beds, others on the floor. This caused one family member to never return. I think she now spends Christmas in the Caribbean.

Back to the rituals. Next comes the gift giving. What a weird conglomeration of packages. Some are wrapped for Christmas, and others are done up for Chanukah. This gift-giving ceremony is where it gets a little iffy for some of us. Let's face it; even one gift per Chanukah night can't compete with receiving a mini-mountain of Christmas gifts. Susan's girls, who are now teenagers, now make their own presents for each person in the extended family. This definitely is the place where this Jewish clan comes dangerously close to stepping over into Christmas territory! Paper strewn everywhere, we move onto the next ritualized event of the evening, picture taking.

Since there is always a non-family member attending the party, they get assigned the role of photographer. Sometimes it is a girlfriend or boyfriend of one of the young adults. Once it was the soon-to-be-intended of my niece. He certainly took his fair share of razing about if a wedding was in the cards and where and when. In fact, there was a wedding the following September. Another year, there was no "stranger," so all the cameras were arranged to go off with their automatic delayed timers. This is such a resourceful clan.

The ending is always the same. We all say that this year's party was the best. As we were about to leave the party this year, I overheard my son say to his cousin that he thought it was time for him to start giving out his own presents. So I anxiously wait to see if he carries out this shift from young-adult child to a gift-giving adult. Hopefully, another generation takes a step to ensuring that the rituals of this family reunion stay in place forever.

THINKING ABOUT PASSOVER

I have frequently written about Passover, focusing on how to make a Seder for the first time; how to redo your Passover plans as the children get older, marry, and bring their own children to the table. The task is to plan a meaningful Seder where everyone feels included in the telling of the story.

So what's left to write about? Gratefulness is on my mind.

Our adult children have started to host some of the holidays. Both have expressed a great desire to do so and have created magnificent Rosh Hashanah, Thanksgiving, and Passover celebrations at their homes with the entire family. As my mother and mother-in-law did for me, I bring them things from my house that they would like to have and I want them to use. I am so grateful to these two women who came before me and taught me how to transfer family traditions through the generations. As I sit at both of our children's tables, I realize how fortunate I am to see how they have incorporated both religious and secular objects from generations past into their homes. Being together with their relatives has been integrated as an important and meaningful part of their lives.

While my son and daughter are doing Jewish holidays, they have not yet taken over all of them all the time. I am not ready to give it all up yet. I think of this time as "the transition years"—everyone gets to do some of the holidays. So what's on the board for this year? Given that we will all be together in a few weeks to celebrate our grandson Joseph's bar mitzvah here in Washington, the New Yorkers will stay in New York, and I will make Seder the first night of Passover for the Washington family. I will certainly miss not being all together this year.

But the story does not end there. The next morning Michael and I will get in the car and drive to New Jersey where my late cousins' children will all be together celebrating the second night of Passover, including our daughter and her family. Our young cousins have thoughtfully included us. When we first moved to Washington, my late cousin Diana and I made all the holidays together. In those days, our parents were often present with us. Now the next generation has taken over our traditions and we are the elders sitting at their tables.

*MARION'S POST SCRIPT:

>Holidays and families are fertile ground for stirring up a field of emotions. What is it like to be the eldest at a holiday celebration hosted by your children? It can feel both good and bad, often at the same time. We are happy because our children have good values, are taking care of their parents, and are continuing the traditions that we started or had passed down to us by our parents. On the other hand, we can experience our own vulnerability at this stage of life, both emotional and physical. We remember when we were doing all the cooking and preparing and managing the stress of the family dynamics, as well as the pressure from work and the need to get the preparations completed so everyone could eat the holiday meal together.

Paying attention to my feelings of getting older, but unsure whether I was ready to give up making the holidays, I decided to once again host lunch on the first day of Rosh Hashanah, as has been my tradition. When my daughter asked me why, I told her that maybe this might be my last hurrah. Right now, I am excited to be planning the menu and thinking about the shopping and the cooking. Who knows, I might regret this decision. But then again, I will have resolved my ambivalence about making the holidays, and that is an excellent solution for now.

WHERE IS BABY MOSES?

Monday night was the first Seder, and twelve of us gathered around the dining room table. I took a deep breath and looked around and saw my husband at the far end with a big smile on his face. He has been working with me on rewriting the Passover narrative. You might say that I have become obsessed with telling the story of Moses from the basket to the wilderness so that my grandchildren understand the story of Moses and the exodus from Egypt. Actually, what I really am obsessed with is making memorable memories for my grandchildren. Last year, I did a little play for our five grandchildren to act out. These are the things that I wished we had done when I was growing up.

The Seders when I was a little girl had their own fun, like my cousin Barry and I drinking too much kosher wine while we were sitting at our end of the table, or the Seder that we went to in Atlantic City, where my sister and I slept in twin beds in a room with a slanted floor. The boardwalk was fun, the Seder was led by a famous cantor, and we were there as a family alone. Then we had some Seders in Florida, where the sun was fabulous after the freezing winter weather in Montreal, our home. The pool was great, Miami Beach was even more fun, but again we were alone as a family. The Seders we had with the Miller family, my parents' best friends, were wonderful. But then my sister got married, the Millers started having numerous grandchildren precluding continuing our Seders together. For a few years, my parents and I were invited to be with my brother-in-law's family at a resort in the mountains. I loved being part of our new extended family.

Marrying Michael meant having big Seders again. His father was one of four brothers, each with his own extended family. The first time I met Michael's sister, Carol, and her family was at a huge Seder at the Ushers' house. After we were married, my in-laws included my parents, which I loved. When we bought our house on Roslyn Avenue, the large dining room begged to have me continue the tradition. Using both of our mothers' recipes, I gathered our families and close friends around the table. We watched our own children learn the Four Questions, read parts of the story in Hebrew, and learn all the songs. I was so proud and grateful.

4—Family and Holidays: Conflict or Resolution?

Moving to Washington again brought new Seders. My cousins, Diana and Milton Engel incorporated us into their Seders. Thus, a new tradition started, and along with cousins, there were close friends, and soon we had huge events with lots of singing, discussions, and noise. When we had thirty people one year, I knew we had reached an absolute maximum.

Oops, I got a little off track here and went down memory lane. Back to our Seder on Monday night. Who else was at the dining room table? There was our son, Douglas, his wife, Libbie, and two of our five grandchildren, Joseph and Tess. Every Seder has its unique experiences. This is the one where Tess said the Four Questions in Hebrew. Joseph said the first question and did what he is so skilled at, "pretending" the rest of the questions. His sense of pride was enormous. Our daughter, Joanna, and her family were in New York, where we were treated by video, to the twins singing the Four Questions. Now all of our five grandchildren have achieved this milestone. Caroline, our fourteen-year-old granddaughter, is now into the "debate and discuss" phase of her development, trying to stump us with her knowledge.

Others at the table include our good friends Wendy and Gerry, who have been coming to our house for all the Jewish holidays, and we love having them. It is very special for me to see them enjoy these gathering. For both of them, I think this is a renewal from their past celebrations as children, which weren't celebratory at all. In addition, Wendy is an outstanding cook and always makes us incredible desserts.

Jane is at the table sitting next to me. She is Libbie's mother and is like a sister to me. We are family, and we look after each other. She moved to Washington six years ago and has never looked back. We are grateful she is here with us. She made the delicious chicken soup.

Audrey, our niece, is at the table next to Jane. She came to Washington thirty years ago to be a Presidential Fellow, never left, and is an intimate part of the family. We have a unique familial relationship, close and reliable. She is always at our table for all holidays unless we are out of town. Her chocolate-dipped strawberries are required or else there is no Seder!

More relatives are included at the table. Josh and Gugu. Josh's father, John, and Michael are first cousins. Josh is with the State Department and has been in DC on assignment that allows them to become permanent members of the "celebrate Jewish holidays at the Ushers" clan. All year, Gugu has been studying Judaism with Rabbi Shira Stutman. Josh has been going along for the ride. Their enthusiasm for the Seder this year was infectious. Josh's specialty was the biblical timeline. They both added content and joy to our gathering. They are leaving for Delhi in June, and Gugu spent time with me telling me how she would like to create a Jewish community for the two of them there so they can continue these celebrations when they are in India. How wonderful is that?!

Back to baby Moses and the play. This year I hid baby Moses in the closet. Tess found him, and then we reenacted Moses being placed by his sister, Miriam, in the bulrushes of the Nile, being found by Pharaoh's daughter, Bithiah, Miriam suggesting that her mother, Yocheved, be the nursemaid, and all of them trotting off to the palace.

As they say, the rest of the Seder was history!

When you are an interfaith family, there are many opportunities for you to create your own traditions. This story outlines the many Seder scenarios, some of which are more fulfilling than others. It is always helpful to evaluate the family's experience after the celebration and pay attention to where you think changes should be made.

FIVE IDEAS FOR CREATING A MEANINGFUL SEDER

Are you in an interfaith relationship or part of an interfaith couple? Have you started preparing for Passover? Keep reading for five interesting approaches to consider as you get started with the upcoming holiday.

A plethora of information is available on the web for everyone to see, read, download, and incorporate. You don't even have to go to a store to buy a coloring book for the children; there is one right there to download and print. *Haggadahs*, from secular to religious and everything in between, can be found throughout the Internet. Given this significant advance with technology, what could I possibly offer that you couldn't find yourself? Actually, I wanted to have some fun with my suggestions, to nudge you along the way of thinking about your involvement with Passover from a different perspective, one that puts you in the active position, making intentional decisions that suit your needs.

So here are my five suggestions for new and creative things you can try this Passover:

1. As a couple or as a family, go to an old-fashioned bookstore or used-books store and look at all the *Haggadahs*. Buy one! Choose the one that you think is the most accessible. Have a cup of coffee at the café and enjoy getting to know your new purchase together.

2. Go home for the Seder. Your parents will be ecstatic! Ask them to prepare their best family recipes and to plan an outrageously fun Seder.

3. If you can't go home, make a Seder with your friends. I know it sounds like a forbidding task, but I promise that you can do this with ease and grace. Start by checking out InterfaithFamily's blog for setting the Passover table and my blog, JewishInterfaithCouples.com, for recipes.

4. Make a batch of Passover chocolate bark. *Smitten Kitchen*'s version, called "Chocolate Caramel Crackers," is an annual favorite, getting wild praise from fans online. It is a great way to turn matzo into a delicious dessert. It is easy to make, and everyone will think you are the most

incredible cook and host! If you make this, you can buy all the rest of the food for the meal. I promise, no one will notice.

5. Make up a play! Last year, I had all my grandchildren participate in a short and sweet play about Moses in the Nile, ending with the ten plagues. Here's your opportunity to be creative. Think about wearing costumes. Throw marshmallows at people when they answer the questions correctly. Start the Seder by hiding Moses in the bulrushes. Feel empowered to tell the Passover story in a new way.

WHAT IS THE HARDEST PART OF PASSOVER FOR INTERFAITH FAMILIES?

The holiday of Passover brings up many issues to think about as we prepare for the festival. We are asked to tell a story—a very scripted story—and one that has many messages for us to heed. We are instructed to change our dishes and clean our houses from top to bottom.

There are questions in the *Haggadah* to answer and so many versions of the text to use. As a result, I sit at one end of the table with many *Haggadot*, each with Post-It notes in it to remind me of a special passage that I would like to include. We always read Mary Oliver's poem "The Season of the Egg," and we read a passage describing Miriam's Cup, something that was not on the Passover table when I was growing up. Then there are the writings from the Labor Zionist, family, children's, social justice, and feminist *Haggadot*. It goes on and on.

When we were blessed with three additional grandchildren at the Seder, I changed the whole thing. I wanted them to understand the Exodus story from beginning to end. Now we start with baby Moses in the Nile. I hide baby Moses in his cradle, and the Seder only can start when they all find him. They all love this new ritual. It is accessible, participatory, and meaningful. The Passover story begs to be adapted and played with. Hopefully, you can come up with your own variations for retelling it, too.

For many years Jean Graubart and I did a Passover "how-to" workshop for interfaith families. I schlepped at least twenty-five different *Haggadot* for them to read and look at. Jean brought Sephardic foods and recipes. Everyone really enjoyed themselves and was most appreciative. However, after one of the sessions, we heard the following, "I love your explanations, and I really learn a lot, but I am the one who will be doing the cooking, and since I am not Jewish, I don't have these recipes, and that is what I really need from both of you."

That led me to compile a Passover recipe book—it is Ashkenazi, reflecting my background, certainly traditional, user friendly and on my website, JewishInterfaithCouples.com. Ultimately, although holidays are often associated with specific foods, they also give us a wonderful opportunity to create new traditions, whether that means adding non-traditional dishes to the menu—maybe something from a non-Jewish partner's family that can be made for Passover, or include readings from different texts. Take this time to make the holiday unique, meaningful, and memorable for your own family.

THREE TIPS TO PERSONALIZE THE PASSOVER AND EASTER HOLIDAYS

When the holidays overlap, havoc can take place. It is hard enough to decide how to navigate your own family's decisions; now you have to think through your parents' expectations, too. As a couple, talk about the issues you are facing, make some choices, and then carry out what you decided to do. After the holidays are over, review your decisions.

Here are three suggestions for interfaith couples to experiment with after celebrating the Passover and Easter holidays. Take some time, sit down together over a cup of coffee or a glass of wine, and have a discussion about the following topics:

1. Did you go to a Seder? If yes, ask each other what you enjoyed about it, and make a list and store it on your phone or computer. Then, together, go over what you did not like about the Seder you attended. Did you both feel welcomed at the Seder you attended?

2. If you did not go to a Seder, talk about why you did not go. Were you too late to find one to go to? Did you not know where to find a Seder? If you are in the DC area, did you know about JConnect.com, which is a local resource for you? EntryPointDC is another source that can help you find a Seder to attend. Many synagogues hold Seders as well. Or were you anxious about attending something that was unfamiliar? Perhaps you didn't go to a Seder because the Jewish partner was afraid to ask the non-Jewish partner. This is a discussion worth having.

3. Did you attend any Easter services or dinners? What did you like about them, and what made you uncomfortable if anything? Add to your list. Did you both feel welcomed at the events?

Your lists will serve as a template for you for next year when it comes time to take action around the Passover and Easter holidays. Together, decide what you want to do in your own home and what you will do with your extended families. With respect and open communication, you can address the issues you face as interfaith couples.

HOW WOULD HOGWARTS HOST A SEDER?:
Inclusive Passover Traditions for the Modern Muggle Jewish Family
Guest Post By Lara Nicolson, Interfaith Engagement Director at the Baltimore JCC

As a child, Passover was my favorite family holiday. We hosted Seders with my extended family, including my two living grandmothers, my aunts, and my three girl cousins, so our celebrations always involved beautiful and confident female voices leading the songs, asking the questions, and making lots of jokes. Our mothers were amazing hosts and cooks and hand-made all the Passover foods from their Lithuanian roots, including herring, *imberlach* (ginger candy), and, of course, matzo ball soup. They would adapt the recipes using ingredients they found in South Africa and would make their own kosher-for-Passover wine with grapes from the local vineyards.

Fast-forward forty years to Baltimore, Maryland, and my immediate and extended family here represents a new Jewish reality—we are diverse in Jewish denominations, nationalities, gender orientation, and faith backgrounds. My husband is not Jewish, and though we are raising our children in a Jewish home, their connections and interests are far from my homogenous upbringing.

Over the last twelve years, we have adapted our Passover traditions to ensure that they are meaningful to everyone. We'll include vegan-friendly dishes, and compare the Passover story to current political issues, while still singing our closing song in Yiddish. This year I even bought the *Hogwarts Haggadah* for my children, hoping it will help them to connect the Exodus story to their current fascination with Harry Potter.

This Passover, I will be with my sister's family and my mother for their more traditional Seder. I know that my interfaith family should be able to participate fully, so I thought I would write a few guidelines that we can all use to make our modern family Seders more inclusive:

1. **Make your Seder interactive to learn from and with the children:** When my children were younger, we had great Passover gimmicks collected from their JCC preschool (plague masks, Velcro Seder plates, and coloring books) and later PJ Library books. Plays and cooking contests were critical tools for keeping them engaged in the Seder and before

dinner. Now, I realize that my husband and other guests new to Passover were learning together with them. Maybe even more than the *Haggadah* and song sheets, the games were informal Jewish education tools. Rabbi Robyn Frisch of InterfaithFamily also has some useful suggestions on how to make your Passover Seder fun for kids of all ages.

2. **Find themes that are meaningful and relevant for all:** For my children, the message of Harry Potter (Moses) and his values of truth and good conquering evil Voldemort (Pharaoh) will resonate at the Seder this year. A few years ago, my cousin created her own version of a Human Rights *Haggadah* that we used to add modern relevance to our age-old "slavery to freedom" story.

3. **Add some pink to your Passover:** Women play an important role in the Exodus story including Moses' mother and sister, Miriam, the midwives, and Pharaoh's daughter, who defies his order to kill the firstborn Jews and saves Moses. For the past few years, my friends and I have attended the Women's Seder hosted by Associated Women in Baltimore, where we gained a new appreciation of the strong women in our lives and their role in our Jewish journeys. It was inspiring to dance with community leaders, female rabbis, and generations of families—while dancing with Miriam's tambourine, drinking from her cup, and adding an orange to the Seder plate—for all who are marginalized in society.

4. **Ask the tough questions:** During the Seder, we are obligated to recite the Four Questions, and we learn about the four sons, including "the one who doesn't know how to ask." All night we are encouraged to engage with the Passover story through thought-provoking questions. For interfaith couples, challenging issues may come to the fore when Easter and Passover fall at the same time. You need to decide how to celebrate, explains interfaith expert Marion Usher. She encourages couples to plan ahead by reflecting on past experiences and making changes that work for their new lives together.

   Now more than ever, the holiday of Passover is symbolic of our obligations to stand up for all who are marginalized, welcome strangers into our community, and make a place at our tables for all.

4

SUMMARY

The task outlined in this chapter is to be purposeful with how you and your spouse celebrate the holidays. The priority, if you are parents, is to agree on how you will raise your children religiously. As you can ascertain from the stories in this chapter, it is your responsibility to clear the channels of communication between the two of you first, and then with each of your extended families. A key part of this process is to decide how the holidays will be celebrated and with whom. As this occurs, you are choosing a path of intention and understanding, a trajectory that yields positive experiences.

The goal is to celebrate the holidays and to create cherished memories.

5

THE NEW JEWISH FAMILY – CONTINUING THE JOURNEY

On June 16, 2017, *eJewish Philanthropy* reported that the clergy of the non-denominational Congregation B'nai Jeshurun in New York would marry interfaith couples. This is a breakthrough. It follows another similar decision made last year by Dorchei Emet, a Reconstructionist synagogue in Montreal, Quebec, where the clergy and congregation made the same bold decision. Conservative Rabbi Amichai Lau-Lavie, of Lab/Shul New York, also declared that he would marry interfaith couples. What a brave decision, since his affiliation with the Conservative movement disallows him of that right!

This is a very exciting time for Judaism. While recent studies focusing on the increase in interfaith marriages and its negative impact on the future generations of Jews predict doom and gloom, there is good reason to contradict such a conclusion. If you broaden the lens to include the views, needs, and opinions of many interfaith families, you will learn how much they want to lead Jewish lives. They want Judaism to be relevant and accessible. I know because I have been listening to these couples and families for twenty-five years. Helping interfaith couples as they solidify their relationships and create their religious lives leads to positive results.

The landscape has changed, and we are all the better for it. The rules are in flux. More of the denominations now understand that to become a totally inclusive Jewish community, the clergy need to marry interfaith couples.

You only have to look at publications in *The Forward*, *Jewish Week*, and *eJewish Philanthropy* to see the plethora of articles on this issue. Hopefully, this public debate results in change. The Reform movement took a progressive perspective and has seen their congregations grow exponentially as a result of this wise decision to marry interfaith couples. Some rabbis have had incredible foresight. In 1962 in Montreal, Rabbi Harry

Stern of Temple Emanuel, informed by his progressive views, married Danny Usher, my husband's cousin, and his Buddhist wife, Sampan.

While the Conservative movement recently acknowledged that it is welcoming to interfaith couples and families, it also declared that Conservative rabbis will not perform interfaith marriages at this time. I believe that performing ceremonies of interfaith couples is mandatory for inclusion to be authentic and complete. Hopefully this decision will be revisited in the future.

There are more resources than ever before available for interfaith couples through classes, workshops, Jewish holiday programs, creative worship, new and innovative religious education programs, Mother's Circle programming for parents of another faith raising Jewish children, subsidized trips to Israel, and a growing acceptance into synagogue and Jewish community life. The Internet has generated multiple possibilities, such as scholarly knowledge, like-minded peer groups, local relevant programs, answers to questions, and locating clergy available for weddings and other life-cycle events. InterfaithFamily.com (IFF), which serves the largest number of interfaith couples and families of any domain, has both an Internet presence and an on-the-ground program of numerous regional directors who perform as programmers, information disseminators, bloggers, and coordinators of community resources. All of the regional directors of IFF now conduct "Love and Religion" workshops in their cities as an ongoing outreach program for interfaith couples.

In Michael Steinhardt's commencement speech to the American Hebrew Academy, he pointed out the positive impact of early intervention for interfaith couples and their decision whether to raise their children as Jews. When a traditional philanthropist like Michael Steinhardt confirms this trend, he helps the traditional mainstream Jewish community to better understand how their inclusiveness of interfaith couples reaps rewards.

Creative outreach programs are thriving. Young rabbis are establishing clusters of worshippers who want a more intimate and community-based practice, working toward greater affiliation with Judaism.

Interfaith families are moving into their own cluster groups. The Edlavitch DCJCC developed a program explicitly encouraging these families to come together for Shabbat and holidays. Graduates of my workshop often continue as a group for the same purpose. The community needs a conduit to help inform them of the resources they might use next, such as nursery schools in the local Jewish institutions. In this way, they won't stay isolated, but will instead attach to the Jewish community.

In rural areas, there is an equally exciting movement of experimental programs focused on reaching out to Jewish families, most of them interfaith. The state I know best, Vermont, now has a full-time director in Burlington, who manages the online forum "Jewish Communities of Vermont." You only have to visit the website to see the vitality and the effort everyone is making to be inclusive. You can hike up a mountain and celebrate Shabbat, go to a mini film festival in Stowe, partake in a spiritual retreat in St. Johnsbury, enjoy a barbecue in Waterbury, or go to a Shabbat service in a traditional synagogue in Manchester. You can even join a recently established intentional Jewish community called Living Tree Alliance in Moretown. Between modern collectives and traditional synagogue life, there is something for everyone. It is an eye-opening experience to see the richness of Jewish experiences available.

I'm always interested in how many of these couples the Jewish population studies have captured in their samples. Yes, the numbers of traditional practicing Jews has declined. However, the number of interfaith couples identified with Judaism has greatly increased. Judaism is alive and very well and teaches us all how to think differently as to what counts as being Jewish.

What's next?

At the turn of the twentieth century, German Jews considered the new wave of immigrants to be inferior. One tactic used to dismiss this group was to discount the Yiddish language they spoke. Reform rabbis felt the need to promote assimilation of immigrants into American culture. How fascinating that in the present day we see the same resistance by the Jewish establishment toward new forms of Jewish practice brought by the influx of interfaith and unaffiliated families who want Judaism, but not according to traditional standards.

There is a parallel between these two movements, one hundred years apart. In the past twenty years, we have seen a positive acknowledgement of Yiddish culture, revived through Yiddish theater and as an academic field of study. Previously dismissed for its novelty, it is now part of mainstream American Judaism. Similarly, broadening the container of Judaism to receive interfaith families and their new ways of practicing has forced the Jewish community to confront what they once discarded.

With all of these new and innovative resources that are available for interfaith couples and families, what has to happen to encourage Jewish choices? Two things: first, acceptance within all formal and informal structures and, second, collaboration in which all stakeholders talk to each other, work together, and suspend their silo approaches to programming. They must manage their competitiveness, and if they can't participate with these values as part of their mission, they should cease to exist, funders should withdraw their financial allocations, and the community should no longer support their activities.

We need new ways of helping families to be Jewish. Presently, we have many creative options for local gatherings, trips to Israel for teenagers, programs for college students, and Israel trips for interfaith couples. With all of these exciting innovations, nothing will thrive unless we have "hand-off" mechanisms in place for interfaith couples and families.

Let me explain. Say a couple is new to a city, they attend a Jewish film festival, and they want to learn about where the Jewish action is in this city. Where do they go? Yes, they will explore the Internet and hopefully gather some information. However, a more laborious, but far more effective way of connecting this couple with the Jewish community is to have a designated professional at the film festival disseminating relevant materials.

Here are more examples of effective "hand-off" procedures. An interfaith family sends its child to a local JCC nursery school. At the conclusion of their time there, they have a meeting with a teacher or director who helps to guide them along their Jewish path. Are they interested in synagogue affiliation, a *chavurah*, or a Jewish day camp? Again, a personal interview will facilitate this family to connect with the appropriate resources for them, followed up with an email, and preferably a phone call to make the introduction. This sounds obvious, and it is. Again, it is labor intensive, but it yields great benefits. But how many groups have this as a "best practices" model for their work?

InterfaithFamily's regional directors, as part of their mission to help guide interfaith families into the local Jewish communities, inform them of resources, make personal connections, recommend available clergy for interfaith weddings, and help them to feel included in their local Jewish community.

Without these connections, creative programming will fall short of the mark. They will serve as silo components existing all alone rather than as part of a continuum fostering immersion.

The second recommendation I want to address is working within Jewish communities to transform the mindset from an either–or stance to one of inclusion. When you give credence to an either-or thought pattern, you fall into polarized opinions of "right or wrong." Little progress is made with this position. Meeting in the middle or somewhere along the spectrum allows for new ways of working together. This requires traditional institutions to work with innovative programs to ensure continuity for all families on the periphery.

These various examples offer ways for people to participate in their religion in their own ways, and in this way, the Jewish community can expand in numbers and in richness of experience and perspective. The new Jewish family is most comfortable with spontaneous actions and intimate experiences.

Stories in this chapter elaborate on the element of how interfaith partners and their families have found inclusion or not, and how that has shaped their Jewish identification.

MAKING EFFECTIVE PROGRAMS FOR INTERFAITH COUPLES AND FAMILIES

The "Statement on Jewish Vitality" falls short. How can we make effective Jewish programs for interfaith couples and families?

Three times each week, nursery school children meet after daycare for a Jewish program called MoEd DC at the Edlavitch DCJCC. The focus is on Hebrew study through immersion and Judaics, balanced with play and homework time. It is a small and effective program that brings young interfaith and unaffiliated families into the Jewish community. Mothers can learn how to bake challah at any of the Whole Food Markets throughout the Washington area, a regular program sponsored by PJ Library. On Sunday mornings, a Jewish focused story-reading session occurs for young children serving interfaith and Jewish families living in the city. These are but a few of the many low-barrier entrance programs into the Washington DC Jewish community, and we need to learn from them.

All these programs stand in sharp contrast to the latest Jewish Vitality report, which saddened me. The solutions it offered were unexciting and are unlikely to have any impact on young interfaith couples. The study suggests that "effective responses are feasible"—but none are proposed specifically for interfaith couples and families.

The survey tells us that 80% of those raised Reform and who married between 2000 and 2003 are intermarried—then this group is never mentioned again. We dare not ignore couples like this if we wish to strengthen our Jewish community. Many of the interfaith couples do want "Jewish," but they want it to be relevant to them, to meet their needs, not ours! It is essential that those of us who work with interfaith couples and families tell a different story, as we know it.

Up until recently, there has been a dearth of creative programming for young interfaith couples and families. Community leaders have been wringing their hands and looking to congregations to fill this void. However, interfaith couples and families tend to be "Jewish-building averse." They cannot afford synagogue dues, they don't particularly enjoy their parents' form of Judaism, and they would prefer to be the creators of their own experiences. Jay Ruderman, president of the Ruderman Family Foundation, said it best when he described this report as a vertical hierarchy devoid of open discussion with solutions imposed by the hierarchy.

Another very successful program created for this interfaith and unaffiliated population is "CityJews PopUp: Shabbat." The target audience is urban families who have made a commitment to city living rather than moving out to the suburbs. In 2015, we held three pop-up Shabbat dinners. Thirty people attended the first one held in my home. Two others were held in a repurposed Wonderbread factory, an edgy space in a recently gentrified area. Each Shabbat dinner drew fifty and seventy people respectively; most of them are interfaith, and others are Jewish and unaffiliated.

Five Jewish agencies and two synagogues came together to sponsor, "City Jews PopUp: Shabbat." The synergy between all of us with similar goals for engagement and meeting these families' needs resulted in a whole new group of families experiencing a central tenet of Judaism, celebrating Shabbat together.

So what is success? What is possible and how can we continue programming for this cohort? What's next? More relevant programming!

With an expanding email list in hand, PJ Library and Love and Religion created two new programs, "Make Room for Latkes" and "Make Room for Matzo." InterfaithFamilyDC, the Jewish Food Experience, Edlavitch DCJCC, and the Jewish Social Service Agency have now partnered with us. Each of these programs has a children's component focusing on a craft project, a social justice component, and a food aspect. Families go home with a bag filled with tokens of Judaism, including Chanukah or Passover prayers, recipes, and a list of community resources. The results were impressive. In the first year, "Make Room for Latkes" had fifty people. Last year, one hundred people participated.

These vignettes represent anecdotal evidence that creative programming draws interfaith families toward Judaism. In talking with the attendees, they feel this is exactly what they want. A cynic might call this "Jewish lite." On the other hand, for many, this is the first time they are attending a program with Jewish content and have put their foot into the Jewish community.

With new and creative ideas, and by exploring relevant ways to involve interfaith families, we can change the community's feeling of helplessness to one of inclusion and vitality. Please, no more reports with old ideas—only interesting ones that help interfaith couples and families imagine being Jewish and see that Judaism adds value to their lives.

Chapter 5—The New Jewish Family—Continuing the Journey

WHAT DO INTERFAITH FAMILIES WANT FROM THE ESTABLISHED JEWISH COMMUNITY?

What do interfaith couples want from the established Jewish community? Some people in the community believe that these couples want to be left alone to manage their religious life by themselves. Others believe that the choice to marry a non-Jewish spouse is a rejection of the Jewish community. I do not believe either to be true.

Since I have been working with interfaith couples and families, I have learned that they want three things from the Jewish community: acceptance, respect for both religious backgrounds, and information. These couples are tired of being excluded and want to be part of the ongoing communal process. This information is very important because it differs from what the elders in the mainstream Jewish community are saying, and it places the burden directly on that community to shift from an exclusive point of view to an extending and inclusive position. Interfaith couples' request, to be accepted, valued, and included, points to new tasks for Jewish institutions: to create a variety of ongoing activities and learning opportunities. It is not enough to run workshops, develop learner Shabbat dinners, and teach classes on how to make a Passover Seder. These programs, while helpful, are limited, and alone they continue to separate interfaith families from the mainstream Jewish community.

The challenge remains how to incorporate interfaith couples and families into the fabric of the already existing institutions. We need to reach out and make a difference. Consider what the Jewish community has done when each wave of new Jewish immigrants came to the United States. Everyone became involved: the social service agencies, the synagogues, the community centers, and the educational institutions. Imagine what might happen if we harnessed that kind of person power for the interfaith couples and families, creating, in effect, a "welcome wagon." It is time to stop wringing our hands and to celebrate the arrival of this wave of "new immigrants."

In addition to acceptance, interfaith couples and families desire to create and structure a religious life that is respectful to both partners' backgrounds. My interfaith workshops have all been given under the auspices of traditional Jewish institutions, namely a Conservative synagogue and the local downtown Jewish Community Center. Given those settings, I assume that each couple wants to have Judaism as part of their religious life; indeed, almost all of the couples with whom I have worked wanted Judaism to be the "lead" religion. Since two people from different religious backgrounds also have two heritages to deal with, even when a conversion takes place, religious programming must be careful to use language that reflects the couples' reality and is respectful of both their heritages. Thus, the notion of "Judaism as the lead religion," still recognizes that more than one religion will be a part of the family's larger religious life. This understanding supports interfaith couples in their struggle to develop a religious life that satisfies them both.

Finally, interfaith couples want information about how to lead a Jewish life. They want to know how to incorporate meaningful rituals into their lives, and thus, they ask questions about finding a rabbi to convert their children, have a *brit milah* (ritual circumcision) for their sons, create a naming ceremony for their daughters, marry them, and participate in all the other life passages marked by religious ritual.

Although many American Jews consider interfaith marriages a problem, I see this as an opportunity. It is up to us, as a community, to help frame the agenda and to present Judaism as the extraordinary and inspiring religion that it is.

BEING RELIGIOUS IS ONLY ONE WAY TO IDENTIFY AS A JEW
A Response to the Pew 2013 Survey of U.S. Jews

It was October 14, 2013. My husband passed me the *New York Times* and said, "You should definitely read this article on page eleven." I saw the headline, "Poll Shows Major Shift in Identity of U.S. Jews," and my heart sank. I knew which direction it was going. Down. That was my first reaction, before I read everyone's responses to the study. Their reactions fell into the "mea culpa" camp.

For the past three decades, there have been studies done on Jewish religious identification and their attachment to the community. Each survey has resulted in more depressing news. Some analysts used such words as "devastating," "dismal," and "disturbing." Another reflected, "I thought there would be more American Jews who cared about religion." Given the disappointment-laden tone of these articles, I wanted to look at the data for myself.

The study states that its key aim is to explore Jewish identity. It identifies remembering the Holocaust and leading a moral and ethical life as central to Jewish identification. The survey, in the report that I read, does not go much further than that. Deconstructing this concept of Jewish identity, beyond traditional religious participation, is key to understanding what our Jewish community looks like today. We have a diverse Jewish community, and individuals see themselves as Jews in a variety of ways, religion being only one of them.

In the 1930s and 1940s in Canada, there was an influx of men and women who were members of the Workmen's Circle movement and identified as Jews, but did not participate in organized Jewish institutions, such as synagogue. As I recall, their Jewish identity was never questioned.

Today, young people are expressing their Jewish identity by participating in the contemporary social justice movement. It has become a home for many Jews who see their identity emanating from leading an ethical and moral life. When these men and women attend a march for a living wage campaign under the banner of Jews United for Justice, they see this activity as core to their Jewish values and their Jewish identity. For them, this is how they express being Jewish.

The increase in Jewish film festivals, Jewish theater, and funds available for Jewish-themed films are all a part of the growing movement to engage Jews through the arts. JCCs are attracting young people through sports, film, theater, food, and *tzedakah* (charity and good deeds) projects. When young families send their children to early childhood education and day care in a Jewish Community Center, they see themselves as expressing their Jewish identity. A new slogan for JCCs could be "Come be Jewish under this huge and inclusive Jewish umbrella!"

In her article *Washington Jewish Week* article "Explaining the Millennials," Rachel Giattino addresses the issue of her age group by saying that they are finding their connection to Judaism in new and innovative ways that reflect the world around them. She informs us that there are ten-plus independent *minyanim* (prayer groups) in the DC area composed of young professionals, and most of these groups function outside of a traditional synagogue structure. These couples and families may never join a synagogue and may choose to educate their children independently. They are creating new ways of being Jewish. They are looking to create their own, new Jewish religious identity, and to not have it imposed by an external institution. Think bottom-up rather than top-down. They are the "new Jewish family."

What does it say about the 1,200 people who gathered on the steps outside Adas Israel congregation on Yom Kippur eve to recite Kol Nidre? They did not need a ticket to participate, and they were not asked if they were members. They came to be part of a prayer service, part of a Jewish communal experience that was different from what they had grown up with.

I have listened to hundreds of young people talk about what Jewish identity means to them. It can be as simple as being a part of a family that is of Jewish ancestry, honoring grandparents who perished in the Holocaust, having a strong belief system, being a part of a social justice effort through a Jewish lens, having an attachment to Jewish culture, or leading an ethical life as described in the Jewish liturgy. Accepting different ways of identifying as a Jew opens up many possibilities.

But why is this not reflected in the survey? If a young couple goes to a "Tot Shabbat" program at a JCC, does this count as raising a Jewish child? Does it count if a group of parents get together for a Chanukah party? Do they count as religious, even though they are not in a conventional structure?

Do they count as having a Jewish identity since they are choosing to celebrate the holidays in an innovative way? They need to be included when surveys are counting who is Jewish.

In her article "And Now Some Good News about the Pew Survey," Bethamie Horowitz offers us a different way of examining the data. It turns out that the American Jewish population has increased to 6.8 million, up from six million. Some point to the Jewish population as reaching almost 7 million. She also states that the rate of intermarriage has pretty much stayed steady since 1990. She goes on to say that 61% of intermarried couples are raising their children as "Jewish or partly Jewish." What happens if there is an effort to engage these couples prior to having children? In my experience, attending a workshop to discuss the issues of intermarriage can have a profound effect. In my last survey of forty couples that took my *Love and Religion* workshop, 87% said they would raise their children as Jews. When models of engagement are readily available, we can affect the outcomes.

I have tried to read as many of the articles as possible about this study. I follow in the steps of distinguished reporters like J. J. Goldberg, Carla Naumburg, and Bethamie Horowitz who have tried to illustrate a more complex and more hopeful picture of our Jewish community. The results of the study do not match my experience. Identifying as a Jew has a different meaning for everyone. If we fail to recognize the many ways we express our Judaism, we will be looking through blinders.

IS OUTREACH EFFECTIVE WITH INTERFAITH COUPLES?
A REVIEW OF FORTY EVALUATIONS OF "LOVE AND RELIGION"
An Interfath Workshop for Jews and their Partners

Currently, there is much discussion about outreach and welcoming interfaith couples and families into the Jewish community. In fact, last month the Jewish Federation of Greater Washington sponsored a community conversation on interfaith families, and next month a similar gathering will occur in New York. Program coordinators, educators, clergy, practitioners, national interfaith organizations, and interfaith families themselves gathered to discuss the issue and examine the outreach efforts.

Many programs are presently being conducted, but little data has been collected about the effectiveness of these intervention programs. Additionally, there have been gaps in the delivery of these products. Providers lose interest, Jewish communal workers pursue other interests, and the outreach effort disappears.

For many years, I have been conducting the workshop "Love and Religion: an Interfaith Workshop for Jews and Their Partners." The target population is seriously dating, engaged, and/or newly married interfaith couples. Over 700 couples have participated in "Love and Religion." As this workshop model is being run in more and more cities, it seemed timely to begin to collect information on the effectiveness of this early intervention workshop.

The evaluation process was constructed to see if the workshop helped these interfaith couples achieve the following goals: 1] they enjoyed the experience of being with other couples facing similar concerns, 2] they learned more about the issues they are facing, and 3] they felt they are not alone in the process. I expected that the couples would bond together, see each other socially, take more courses, and feel a greater attachment to the Jewish community. The ultimate goal is that the couples choose Judaism as the lead religion in the home and that they raise their children as Jews.

The evaluation also asked questions to determine if attendance at this workshop increased the possibility of the couples deciding to establish a Jewish home, whether they would identify with the Jewish community, and to hear what other type of services and programs they would find attractive and interesting.

The analysis of the evaluations demonstrated the effectiveness of a consistent outreach program. All participants except for one said they would recommend the workshop to their friends. The majority agreed that the workshop met their expectations and for most of the participants, the workshop was seen as helpful in gaining understanding of the issues they were dealing with. One person disagreed.

When looking at the response to the question "What did you like most about the workshop?" the answers, to a fault, were "hearing from other couples who are similar" and "learning from each other's experiences." Since one of the assumptions was expecting that the couples would enjoy finding people in like situations, the number of those meeting up together should reflect that idea. One class had already established an email group after the first session. They made plans to go out for drinks after the workshop ended. In another class, two couples did spend time together. Many of the classes in the past formed their own interfaith couples group. When a reunion was held several years ago, one entire cohort, except for one couple, came to the event "en masse." The missing couple was at the hospital, having a baby!

When the participants were asked "Has the workshop changed any of your opinions about any topic we discussed in the sessions?," they had a lot to say. Some realized that they needed to have more dialogue about religion between themselves as a couple. Many of the Jewish partners, especially the men, felt they had to take on more responsibility for the transmission of Judaism in their homes other than just "I want Jewish children." Others felt they became calmer about the whole issue. They felt they now had some "emotional space" in which they could have a conversation. One person said, "It helped push me to accept and better understand things out of my comfort zone."

These findings in my study, particularly that 87% of the couples will raise their children as Jews, are both exciting and promising. I believe that the mission of the model, providing a safe and supportive environment for open discussion of these complicated issues and encouraging Jewish choices, helps couples to feel welcomed into the Jewish community and to raise their children as Jews. On occasion, some couples terminate their relationship and/or leave the workshop because it becomes clear that during the course of being in the workshop, one or the other realizes the importance of their own religion and that compromise is not possible.

The last topic covered in the evaluation focuses on if the couples want anything more from the Jewish community. The answer is an unqualified "yes," they want more! They want courses in Judaism, guidelines on how to make holidays, interfaith learners' Shabbat dinners, trips to Israel, cooking classes, tips on how to choose a welcoming synagogue and find a conversion class, and, my favorite answer of all, a "challah-bread home-delivery service."

These results suggest that a workshop like "Love and Religion: An Interfaith Workshop for Jews and Their Partners" is an effective entry-level outreach program for interfaith couples. It is the first step on their journey. It bonds them together, they enjoy being among their peers, they become more comfortable within the Jewish community, and it helps them to feel supported in their decision to raise their children as Jews. All of these findings underscore the pivotal importance for the Jewish community to continue to increase the opportunities for the incorporation of interfaith couples and families into the greater Jewish community.

Chapter 5—The New Jewish Family—Continuing the Journey

THIS IS WHAT OUTREACH LOOKS LIKE – CITYJEWS POP UP SHABBAT

Seventy people—families, couples, young children and babies—all gathered together to celebrate Shabbat. Who are these people, and why is this unique? These are "City Jews" who have made a commitment to live in the city, even in parts of the city where none of us veteran Washingtonians would have dared to go five years ago. Did I say five years—how about two years ago? These young couples are committed to urban living, including using public transportation, constructing community, and sending their children to public school. Many work in the social justice world and want to actively participate in making the world a better place.

At 6 p.m., the first people began to arrive. After a few kinks were resolved—such as getting the people into the locked building!—the crowd assembled, and the excitement in the room was electric with children running up and down the halls, parents chatting with each other, and introductions being made. This is exactly the buzz we were hoping for. Some people knew each other, some recognized their neighbors, some didn't know anyone, and others came out of pure curiosity. But they were all there to have Shabbat dinner with a likeminded community.

After an initial welcoming, Rabbi Hannah Goldstein, from Temple Sinai, led us in the Shabbat prayers and offered a *dvar Torah* on the importance of building community. As people were eating dinner, the children heard a story read by Bini Silver of the DCJCC, and then they went on to create an art project with Sarah Rabin Spira of PJ Library. Each child went home with a pillowcase in hand decorated with the *Shema* prayer.

One of the unique aspects of this experience is that seven community groups came together to create this dinner: Adas Israel, a Conservative congregation, Temple Sinai, a Reform congregation, the Jewish Food Experience, PJ Library, the DCJCC, Love and Religion, and Sixth & I Historic Synagogue.

"CityJews PopUp: Shabbat" is a perfect way for Jewish and interfaith families to experience and celebrate a meaningful Shabbat together. Members of this urban population want something Jewish, but are not yet ready for institutional attachment. It is my hope that through these "pop-up" Jewish experiences, we will be supportive to a large number of young families in their search for new Jewish experiences. Following this event, I received a call from someone requesting that we do a "CityJews PopUp: Shabbat" on Capitol Hill, another urban neighborhood in Washington!

ENGAGING INTERFAITH COUPLES THROUGH THE ARTS

Love and Religion, Theater J, Adas Israel Congregation's Beit Midrash, the JCC of Northern Virginia, and the Washington DCJCC co-sponsored a reading of the play *Love, Faith and Other Dirty Words*, written by Kent Stephens. The play is about interfaith couples and the critical issues they face. The purpose of the production was to reach out to interfaith couples through the performing arts. It was the first time such an event was undertaken in our community and five agencies worked together to make it happen. We also collaborated with the New Center for Arts and Culture of Boston, whose mission is to have this important play read in cities all over the country and have interfaith couples use this medium to further explore the decisions they were in the process of making.

While I had read the play a few times, I was unprepared for my intense involvement with the actors as they took on these roles leading up to the show. The content of the play emerged from the playwright's discussions with interfaith couples in various combinations of religions, including Jewish, Christian, Muslim, and Hindu. The potential of this play for dialogue among people of many faiths is enormous.

After each performance we held "talk-backs," and each night was a very different conversation. In leading the discussion after the performance at Adas Israel Congregation, I assisted the actors in a further exploration of their character's religious positions. We plumbed their experiences of being in their particular role and focused on what they were feeling in their character. It was fascinating to have them tell us when they were beginning to change their minds about their religion—sometimes more collaboratively with their partner and sometimes more internally driven.

On the second evening, the "talk-back" was moderated by a panel comprising Ari Roth, the artistic director of Theatre J; Jeff Dannick, the executive director of the Northern Virginia JCC; and I. If the first night was described as "micro," meaning the discussion focused on the couples themselves, the second night explored the "macro" possibilities for this play. Ari set the stage by asking, "How can we could use this play to foster an open dialogue with couples of many faiths? How can we explore where we meet and where we differ, and can we attempt to understand our common values and explain our core-meaning systems to each other?" These questions captivated the audience and the conversation went far beyond the material presented in the play. We all left the evening feeling stimulated with a multitude of complicated thoughts and with homework to do. The lingering question was: "How do we bring together people of different faiths and explore opportunities?"

This artistic endeavor, *Love, Faith and Other Dirty Words*, proved to be a perfect vehicle for bringing young people together to talk about their experiences as an interfaith couple and then as a community with different religions living side by side.

THE WONDER TWINS – A TALE DEMONSTRATING A WELCOMING COMMUNITY

A few years ago I received an invitation to Asher and Abigail's first birthday party. These twins are also known as the "Wonder Twins." Why? Because they were born very early in gestation, and they were now going to celebrate their first birthday. They survived, they were thriving—it was a miracle! I couldn't wait to go to this celebration.

I walk in the door of the townhouse where the party was being held, not expecting to see anyone I knew except for the parents. I immediately bump into Rabbi Stephanie Bernstein, a kindred spirit. I am curious about why she is here, but I wait until we catch up on news with each other. Then Stephanie says to me, "Oh, you must be here because the parents took your class!" I answer, "Yes." She continues with, "Well, I am here because I did their wedding, and I did the baby naming and the *brit milah*." We both hug each other and enjoy this precious moment.

Allow me to deconstruct this experience. At that moment, Stephanie and I both realized the impact we had on this family through our interfaith work. The parents attended my workshop when they were engaged. Since my workshop is an entry-level outreach program, I often don't hear about the couple again. So when I saw Stephanie, and she told me of her connection with the family, both of us saw the fruits of our labor and passion: bringing Judaism to interfaith couples.

This vignette clearly indicates how a family benefits from a system of continuous support by different parts of the Jewish community. This couple availed themselves to many of the offerings, such as a rabbi who performed interfaith marriages, a workshop to address interfaith issues, and a welcoming JCC. They now see themselves as part of the Washington Jewish community. The twins are taking swimming lessons at the Washington DCJCC, the agency where the parents took their first interfaith program. This family looked for resources and found them. Their Jewish journey is a success story.

*MARION'S POST SCRIPT

    A few years after the birth of the twins, their father decided to convert to Judaism.

PRESENTATION TO THE BOARD OF THE JEWISH FEDERATION OF GREATER WASHINGTON

A POSITION PAPER
Where We've Been and Where we Need to Go

It is impressive that the Federation has put this important topic front and center to be addressed by our greater Jewish community. This population of interfaith couples and families requires a number of services to meet their needs. We require multiple resources and a coordinated effort. All those who are involved must collaborate with each other and hand off families to the appropriate place. Cooperation leads to inclusion.

The content of your proposal covers the broad scope of the issue. However, it is now time to think beyond the position of "welcoming and engaging" and concentrate on *creativity* and *incorporation*. Only then can we authentically call ourselves an inclusive community.

I would like to see us focus on new and creative approaches that have been tried elsewhere. For example, in *Tablet Magazine*, Nextbook's online magazine, on October 19, 2011, Eli Sanders wrote an article about Portland, Oregon. The article focused on their Jewish population census results and some "out-of-the-box" outreach programs they had initiated. They held a "Shabbat in the Park," which included a fun activity, a Shabbat meal, and a religious service. It would be very interesting to learn about this creative project and to hear about the results, both positive and negative, that emerged out of this project.

By incorporation, I am referring to seeing interfaith couples identify with the Jewish community through its formal institutions and its informal structures. This assumption then informs our programming efforts. Presently, there are many outreach efforts being conducted here in the Washington, DC area. Specifically, "Love and Religion: An Interfaith Workshop for Jews and Their Partners," is an entry-level program run on a regular basis at the Edlavitch DCJCC. This captures the young dating, engaged, and newly married couple. The purpose of the workshop is to help couples address their interfaith issues. It encourages Jewish choices. We also have "City Jews: Pop-up Shabbat" and "City Jews: Pop-Up Havdalah" programs with an educational, religious and celebration component to the event.

Chapter 5—*The New Jewish Family—Continuing the Journey*

You are all aware of the many programs being offered through our synagogues. "Introduction to Judaism," and "Stepping Stones" are two welcoming programs done in many Reform congregations. Jewish Outreach Institute has a "Mother's Circle" curriculum, which is a very effective way of incorporating the non-Jewish partner, mostly mothers and some fathers, into the Jewish community. The groups are held in synagogues and JCCs.

Synagogues and the JCCs in the area offer a variety of programs welcoming interfaith couples and families. All these programs provide knowledge, possible friendship, and help for interfaith couples on their journey of Jewish identification and facilitate their being incorporated into the Jewish community. The programs are plentiful, but the coordination is missing.

These many outreach efforts, taken together or in continuum, can be considered "best practices." We can look to Rabbi Ari Moffic, who is running the InterfaithFamily outreach program in greater Chicago and is using a five-point approach to incorporate interfaith couples and families into the Chicago Jewish community. She started with a "Love and Religion" workshop and now organizes groups several times a year. Additionally, she is setting up a parenting program specifically for interfaith families. InterfaithFamily has also built in an evaluation component, assessing the success of this entire effort. It would be helpful to have Rabbi Moffic present her "best practices" work to our Federation and share her experiences of what works and what doesn't. In this way, we, as a group, can look at how we get interfaith couples to attach, identify, and belong to the greater Jewish community.

After "welcoming and engaging," do we know what our interdaith families want next? On Yom Kippur, I bumped into a young woman who had attended my workshop at the DCJCC several years ago. I was delighted to see her, her two-year-old daughter, and her husband attending services at Adas Israel. She immediately said to me, "Marion we need your help" and asked, "What do we do next?" I wanted to find out what she meant so we arranged to meet.

After catching up and meeting for a couple of hours, she said she needed skills to get through what she called "the next phase." She herself had studied at a Jewish day school. She did not need knowledge, but she wanted language to explain to her husband that Shabbat was an important experience for her and why. She wanted him to understand that Judaism was more than a religion; it was also a culture and a civilization, and she needed the words to express her thoughts. So we concluded that we would both think about what she had presented to me, and we would try to see if there were other interfaith families who felt the same way. I said I would think of a "next steps" class for interfaith couples who had taken my workshop and who now had children. She said she would talk to the rabbi at the congregation where her daughter was attending nursery school and see if she would lead a discussion group to help these families build their Jewish identity. Here is an opportunity to have this young woman build the agenda where she and her family feel comfortable. This is bottom-up programming, a necessary process to engage interfaith families.

I would also like to see the Federation address the gaps in services. That is, how do we guide these couples with young children to our Jewish nursery schools? Research has already demonstrated the positive effect of a Jewish nursery school experience on the child and the family's attachment to a Jewish identity. Attending a Jewish nursery school fosters the family's incorporation into the Jewish community. Additionally, why are we not running enough Jewish day care centers in our Jewish organizations, a much-needed resource which would attract young families into the Jewish community and then, hopefully, into our already established Jewish groups?

I look forward to working with you on how we move from welcoming to incorporating interfaith families into the greater Jewish community.

5

SUMMARY

Intermarriage among the Jewish people is not a new phenomenon. Historically, this has been going on for a very long time. Let's start with the Bible for some examples. Moses married Tzipora, a Midianite. Her father, a priest, was a founder of the Druid faith. Solomon had 700 wives, including one of Pharaoh's daughters. David had multiple wives, many of whom were of another faith. While some of these myths may be apocryphal, it appears that our forefathers had no compunction to intermarry.

In our contemporary history as the Jewish people, we have seen a complete ban against intermarriage. The marriage to a non-Jew was regarded as verboten. The religious ritual of sitting *shiva* for an intermarried child, as if he or she had died, was the usual and customary practice to sever the familial relationships. The general population was privy to this mourning ritual done by Tevye in the popular play *Fiddler on the Roof*.

This negative attitude toward intermarriage has prevailed into the twenty-first century, much longer than some of us hoped it would. Many still see marrying out as reprehensible, and the Jewish community still worries that intermarriage will result in a decreasing number of Jews.

Where are we now, in 2018?

To be seen as an authentic inclusive Jewish community, all spouses of another faith must be included in our homes, our synagogues, and in our Jewish communal institutions. Acceptance, not rejection, is a necessary requisite to keep Jewish families united. Acceptance represents a path toward the growth of Judaism and the Jewish people. All my efforts are toward moving interfaith couples and families from the periphery into the center. The stories in this book demonstrate how this is accomplished.

Jews have a strong capacity for resilience. We have survived expulsion, pogroms, the Holocaust and many other horrific tragedies. The intersection of resilience, creativity, and collaboration bring hope. With hope, we can build stronger ties, by which we can anticipate confidence in our survival and increasing our numbers.

APPENDIX

A DESCRIPTION OF "LOVE AND RELIGION: A WORKSHOP FOR JEWS AND THEIR PARTNERS"

Created by Marion Lazar Usher, PhD

Over twenty-five years ago, I developed a workshop in which interfaith couples could visualize and learn how to construct a religious life together. From my clinical experience, I knew that early intervention could make an enormous difference. Each workshop became a process, one where the couples could be vulnerable with each other and learn how to co-create a religious life together. They also learned how to talk to each other and to members of their families. In the sessions, couples revealed their worries, their concerns, and their dilemmas. They asked each other questions. They saw other couples who wanted to talk about the same things they did; they did not feel alone.

Today, "Love and Religion: A Workshop for Jews and Their Partners" is organized around four ninety-minute sessions held in four successive weeks. Each session has a theme. The first session is called "Falling in Love – Managing the Elephant in the Living Room." Here I ask each couple to tell the group how and under what circumstances they met. After that, each person of the couple shares with the group what attracted them to their partner. Finally, each couple discusses when religion first came up in the relationship. This step-by-step process allows the couples to see religion as a part of their relationship instead of a single, overriding issue.

The second session, "Remembering Our Past – Imagining Our Future," underscores the uniqueness of each interfaith couple. Each partner in a couple brings their own religious background into the relationship. Together, they build a new religious life, being respectful of their families of origin and, at the same time, deciding what they want for themselves.

I ask each couple to share their religious upbringing, what they found meaningful in their family's religious practice and beliefs, and what they want to bring forward. The purpose of this exercise is to help each partner to listen attentively and respectfully to the other. As they hear one another, they also have the opportunity to imagine how they can or cannot knit their visions together.

The third session is "Co-Constructing a Religious Identity – and What About the Children?" The main focus here is on identity, with two central themes: family-of-origin issues and deciding how religion will be practiced in the home when their children arrive. This dialogue among the partners themselves helps them to address their desires and their disagreements. The hope is that they will see how they can create a religious life together.

Each couple is asked to describe how they conceive of their own religious identity. Here the discussion includes values, ethics, heritage, belief systems, and religious practices. Each person addresses their own religious identity and how the religious practice in the family shaped their personal religious identity. Within a framework of mutual acknowledgement and respect, each individual is encouraged to express their own thoughts, feelings, and beliefs.

Then, each couple focuses on how they see themselves raising their children. This is the point at which I invite the group to explore different scenarios. Some couples have decided to raise their children Jewish, others will say that they want to integrate both religions, and some are still undecided. Quite often, one partner has held back as to how they really feel, worrying that their wishes will not be well received by the other. The discussion can be tense as well as relieving. The richness of the discussion allows room for people to shift and to change their minds.

A central component of this discussion is the concept of loss—something often keenly felt from the beginning of the courtship. When dating someone of another faith, each person is in a situation in which difference is present and sameness is lost. It can be in the subtle nuances where this is first experienced: an anglicized Yiddish word such as *mensch* may not be understood, while traditions of Lent may not be known by a Jewish partner. Since Christianity is the dominant religion in the Western world, the nuance for the Jewish partner is less frequent, but equally strong.

When couples decide how they will raise their children religiously, loss is always a part of the experience. Acknowledging the presence of loss in intermarriage brings another elephant into the living room. Couples can imagine that none of this matters and that all will be well, which, of course, it can be. But when the obstacles are identified and dealt with, resolution and reconciliation become possible. Identifying loss as a component of the process helps clear the emotional pathways.

In the fourth session, I teach the couples the essential components of having an emotionally healthy marriage, "Living Happily Ever After – Learning Skills to Manage the Relationship."

Here I discuss two models, which provide frameworks for couples to consider how the psychological dynamics function in their relationships.

The first model is based on the concepts of attachment and autonomy. I explain these two concepts and how they operate in a relationship. Attachment exists between two people when each feels he or she can rely unconditionally on the other person. It is an emotional state in which each partner understands that they are available for the other. Each person belongs to the other.

Autonomy is defined as all that we do to take care of ourselves. It refers to how we function in our family and work lives, how we manage our internal life, and how we take charge of our independence.

Using a Venn diagram, overlapping circles represent the "attachment" part of the relationship, and the two outside parts of the logo represent each person's capacity for "autonomous behavior." If the circles totally overlap, then the relationship will be smothered, and there will be no air to breathe. If the two circles do not even touch, the two people are living in a relationship with little intimacy between them.

The second model is based on the work of Dr. John Gottman. His research identifies which processes are malignant to a marriage, which are helpful, and what couples can do to improve their relationship.

These two models, characterizing how healthy couples relate, consistently yield fruitful conversations. In the participants' efforts to apply these newly learned skills and concepts, they often first focus on their parents' mode of operating. As they become more comfortable with revealing their own issues, they go on to talk about their own dynamics. They appreciate having these new tools and skills for looking at their own modes of operating. Often this is their favorite session!

At the end of the session, I leave fifteen minutes for any questions they might have, as well as time for a wrap-up of their experience in the workshop.

Some questions I pose include:
Did the workshop meet your expectations? What did you find particularly helpful? What did you find unhelpful? Did your ideas change? How did they change? What else do you want from the JCC?

Between sessions, the couples have homework assignments. They are expected to have a conversation with someone they have been hesitant to talk with in their families, or they can choose to talk to each other about something they have been avoiding. In addition, they are encouraged to go to the Internet and search for something new about interfaith marriage or religion of which they have no knowledge. You can see how each couple watches the responses of the others. Their glances at each other, or their avoidance of each other's gaze, tells me how they are processing the information. By the end of the last session, the group has coalesced. They leave wanting more classes and communal experiences, such as Shabbat dinners, holiday celebrations, and "Introduction to Judaism" classes. Often, they go on as a group and meet regularly by themselves.

The goal of the workshop is to have a safe place where interfaith couples can explore their religious backgrounds, their conflicts, and their capacities to create solutions for themselves. Through the workshops, interfaith couples feel affirmed and know that they are not alone. The strategy of inclusion is one of the basic tenets of this work. Encouraging Jewish choices for interfaith couples is another.

The workshop is now run on an ongoing basis in over ten cities in the United States and Canada. It is the first entry-point program conducted by InterfaithFamily.com's regional directors. While studies of couples who experienced no interfaith counseling suggest that intermarriage is a deterrent to raising Jewish children, pointing to only 33% raising their children Jewish (National Jewish Population Survey, 2000, Pew study 2013), a survey of couples who took my workshop revealed that over 87% of graduates have declared their home to be Jewish and to raise their children as Jews (*eJewish Philanthropy*). Meeting couples where they are, offering relevant Jewish experiences and an early intervention model, and promoting inclusion all contribute to making more Jews in the world.

In 2009, I produced a film, *Love and Religion: An Interfaith Workshop for Jews and Their Partners*, illustrating the workshop with a complementary manual, which guides rabbis and Jewish communal workers to facilitate interfaith workshops in their own communities. The film premiered in 2009 at the Washington Jewish Film Festival.

The film and manual can be viewed on my website: www.JewishInterfaithCouples.com

In 2016, the workshop was a semi-finalist for the Lippman Kanfer Foundation for Living Torah Award.

FURTHER READING

Abramowitz, Yosef, and Silverman, Rabbi Susan. *Jewish Family and Life, Traditions, Holidays and Values, for Today's Parents and Children.* New York: Golden Books, 1997.

Bellin, David. *Choosing Judaism: An Opportunity for Everyone.* New York: The Jewish Outreach Institute, 2000.

Cowan, Paul, and Cowan, Rachel. *Mixed Blessings: Marriage Between Jews and Christians.* Garden City, NY: Doubleday, 1987.

Crohn, Joel. *Mixed Matches: How to Create Successful Interracial, Interethnic, and Interfaith Relationships.* New York: Fawcett Columbine, 1995.

Diamant, Anita, and Cooper, Howard. *Living a Jewish Life.* New York: Harper Collins. 1991.

Diamant, Anita. *The New Jewish Wedding, Revised.* 1985. Fireside, New York: Scribner, 2001.

Diamant, Anita. *The New Jewish Baby Book.* Woodstock, VT: Jewish Lights, 1994.

Einstein, Stephen J., and Kukoff, Lydia. *Every Person's Guide to Judaism.* New York: UAHC Press, 1989.

Friedland, Ronnie, and Case, Edmund, ed. *The Guide to Jewish Interfaith Family Life: An InterfaithFamily.com Handbook.* Woodstock, VT: Jewish Lights Publishing, 2001.

Gottman, John. *Why Marriages Succeed or Fail and How You Can Make Yours Last.* New York: Simon and Schuster, 1994.

Gross, David C. *Why Remain Jewish?* New York: Hippocrene Books, Inc., 1994.

Glaser, Gabrielle. *Strangers to the Tribe: Portraits of Interfaith Marriage.* New York: Houghton Mifflin Co., 1997.

Kaplan, Jane. *Interfaith Families: Personal Stories of Jewish-Christian Intermarriage.* Santa Barbara, CA: Praeger Publishers, 2004.

Keen, Jim. *Inside Intermarriage: A Christian Partner's Journey Raising a Jewish Family.* Springfield, NJ: Behrman House, 2017.

Kukoff, Lydia. *Choosing Judaism.* New York: UAHC Press, 1981.

Mayer, Egon. *Love and Tradition: Marriage between Jews and Christians.* New York: Plenum Press, 1985.

McGinty, Keren. *Still Jewish: A History of Women and Intermarriage in America.* New York: New York University, 2009.

McGinty, Keren. *Marrying Out: Jewish Men, Intermarriage and Fatherhood.* Bloomington, IN: Indiana University Press, 2014.

Olitzsky, Kerry M. *Making a Successful Jewish Interfaith Marriage: The Jewish Outreach Institute Guide to Opportunities, Challenges, and Resources.* Woodstock, VT: Jewish Lights, 2001.

Personk, Judy, and Remsen, Jim. *The Intermarriage Handbook: A Guide for Jews and Christians.* New York: Arbor House, William Morrow, 1988.

Thompson, Jennifer. *Jewish on Their Own Terms.* Rutgers, NJ: Rutgers University Press, 2014.

Usher, Marion. "Working with Interfaith Couples and Families: Emerging Themes." AFTA Annual Meeting. February 2001.

Usher, Marion. "Interfaith Families Need Exclusive Programs." Originally published in *Washington Jewish Week*, reprinted on *www.InterfaithFamily.com*.

Usher, Marion. "What Interfaith Families Want from the Established Jewish Community." *www.InterfaithFamily.com*, April 2001.

Usher, Marion. "What Makes a Family Jewish or What is a Jewish Family? Critical Issues Facing Interfaith Couples and Families." *Sh'Ma*, February 20, 2003.

Wolfson, Ron. *The Art of Jewish Living: The Shabbat Seder.* New York: The Federation of Jewish Men's Clubs, 1985.

WEBSITES

JewishInterfaithCouples.com (including Marion's recipes)

AdasIsrael.org (for videos of interfaith families' Jewish journeys)

Center for Jewish History, cjh.org

EdmundCase.com

InterfaithFamily.com

Jewniverse.com

JewishFoodExperience.com

Kveller.com

MyJewishLearning.com

ACKNOWLEDGEMENTS

Like everyone else who has tried to write their first book, I underestimated the amount of labor it takes to produce the manuscript. Without the support of many people, I would not have completed this project.

Thank you…

To my children, Joanna Usher Silver, David Silver, Douglas Usher, and Libbie Rifkin, who have supported my passion about my work throughout all these years. They are raising our five magnificent grandchildren with Judaism inside of their hearts and souls.

To Michael Usher, my husband, who has stood by my side watching me as I developed my workshop, made my DVD, and then wrote this book. He has read all my writing, rarely offering any comments other than "That's good" for fear of being challenged! When I showed him the first printed version of the book his tone changed to one of celebration and I understood that as his relief that this project was finally on its way to completion!

Without Anita Hoffman, my assistant, there would be no book. She took charge of the computer, of all the technical aspects, she read every word on each page many times, she edited my words, she held my hand, which I especially needed when we discarded some of the stories, and she was my rock whenever my worries moved into ascendency.

Cathy Newman is responsible for shaping my words. She taught me how to write a sentence, a paragraph, and a chapter. I will always be her student, and she will always be my teacher. The size of her heart and her incredible skill as a writer and editor made her an inspirational mentor. When she decided that she really didn't like my title, she quickly sent me some new ones to consider. She was right.

When I asked Merav Levkowitz, who has been managing my website to do the copyediting, I knew that I was in good hands. I am lucky to be the recipient of her skills. Merav has brought me into the twenty-first century with our ongoing relationship between two cities, Washington, DC, and Tel Aviv, Israel, and, of course, on the computer.

My good friends Phyllis Hanfling and James Schwartz have been editing for me since I was working on my doctoral dissertation. Both of them have an acute sense of sentence construction, correct tenses, and how to put the paragraphs in the right order. I am so grateful to both of them for making meaning out of my thoughts and words.

Betty Clayman-DeAtley whose patience and willingness to teach knows no bounds and who magically transformed my ideas into this wondrous book, thank you.

Sarah Rabin Spira, Paul Entis, Sara Shalva, Darya Watnick, and Rabbi Sarah Tasman have all been partners with me in creating new programs. They are a part of the exciting new cohort of Jewish communal workers who understand that an inclusive community brings enormous gains to the greater Jewish community.

For many years, Jean Graubart, as director of the Leo and Anna Smilow Center for Jewish Living and Learning at the DCJCC, built a yearly curriculum of programs focused on couples and families in which they could learn about Judaism. She coordinated with the film, theater, literature, and early childhood education centers, creating a home where interfaith couples and families felt welcomed and included in all aspects of the institution. She partnered with me as we constructed an inclusive community.

Edmund Case, an incredible mensch, and the first CEO of InterfaithFamily has championed all my efforts as I developed my workshop, "Love and Religion," made my DVD, and tried out new and innovative programming. We have traveled this road together over many years.

Jodi Bromberg, the CEO of InterfaithFamily, has put interfaith families as the first item on everyone's agenda. She has grown the organization, and it is now the major player on the national scene for interfaith families. With multiple Regional Directors in place, interfaith families are receiving the help they require. I am grateful for her support of all my work and especially when she flew to DC when I was honored by the Edlavitch DCJCC for "Love and Religion: A Workshop for Jews and Their Partners," which had been conducted consistently for the past twenty years.

To my synagogue, Adas Israel Congregation, where the clergy members have not only supported my ideas and my efforts, but have also provided me with a home for my work and for my spiritual life. Rabbi Jeffrey Wohlberg asked me to conduct my first workshop in 1994. Rabbi Gil Steinlauf listened to my ideas and gave me carte blanche to try anything that would make our synagogue a more inclusive congregation. It was there that I held my first grandparent group. Our congregation is now blessed with our Co-Senior Rabbis Lauren Holtzblatt and Aaron Alexander whose eyes and hearts are open to everyone. To walk with them is an honor. They embrace my ideas and support all my efforts.

Thank you to all the individuals, couples, and families who have shared their beautiful stories so others can learn from their experiences.

Thank you to all my friends and family, who have listened to me over the years and challenged some of my ideas, yet have always been there for me.

MARION L. USHER, PhD

Dr. Marion Usher is the creator of "Love and Religion: An Interfaith Workshop for Jews and Their Partners." With her cohort of over 700 couples, she explores the issues interfaith couples need to address as they co-create the religious life of their new family. Her workshop is now being conducted in ten cities across the United States and Canada. Her DVD and manual illustrating her workshop model premiered at the Washington DCJCC Film Festival in 2009.

Her interfaith workshop was a semi-finalist for the Lippman-Kanfer Prize for Applied Jewish Wisdom in 2016.

Dr. Usher consults with interfaith couples and families, synagogues, JCCs, and other Jewish organizations, helping them to develop creative programming for interfaith couples and families and on her website, www.JewishInterfaithCouples.com, where she blogs on issues related to interfaith marriage. Her articles have appeared in *The Jewish Week* (Washington and New York), *InterfaithFamily.com*, *Sh'ma*, *eJewish Philanthropy*, *The Washington Post*, *The Washingtonian*, *On Faith*, and *Jewish Food Experience*.

She partners with other Jewish communal groups in Washington, DC, to create new outreach programs for interfaith families, which can be replicated in other cities. Some are "Make Room for the Matzo," "Make Room for the Latkes," and "City Jews: Pop Up Shabbat." Each program has a Jewish activity for the children and a discussion component for the parents.

Dr. Usher is a Clinical Professor in the Department of Psychiatry, at George Washington University School of Medicine and Health Sciences, where she supervised residents in psychiatry and helped design the Family Therapy curriculum.

Marion L. Usher, PhD
www.JewishInterfaithCouples.com
marionusher@aol.com
C: 202-236-9495

CPSIA information can be obtained
at www.ICGtesting.com
Printed in the USA
BVHW04s1914060418
512704BV00003B/9/P